S0-ANP-722

CAPE EDITIONS 8

General Editor: NATHANIEL TARN

Lichtenberg, Georg Christoph

Lichtenberg: Aphorisms & Letters

Translated and edited by
Franz Mautner and Henry Hatfield

JONATHAN CAPE
THIRTY BEDFORD SQUARE
LONDON

838.608
Lichtenberg

First published in Great Britain 1969
by Jonathan Cape Ltd, 30 Bedford Square, London, WC1
© 1969 by Franz H. Mautner and Henry Hatfield
This book is an abridged version of *The Lichtenberg Reader* (Beacon, Boston, U.S.A.)
© 1959 by Franz H. Mautner and Henry Hatfield

S B N Paperback edition 224 61286 7
Hardback edition 224 61287 5

Condition of Sale

This book is sold subject to the condition that it
shall not, by way of trade or otherwise, be lent,
re-sold, hired out, or otherwise circulated
without the publisher's prior consent in any form
of binding or cover other than that in which it is
published and without a similar condition being
imposed on the subsequent purchaser.

Printed and bound in Great Britain
by Richard Clay (The Chaucer Press), Ltd
Bungay, Suffolk

Contents

INTRODUCTION:
LICHTENBERG ON HIMSELF

Character of a person of my acquaintance.

His body is so constituted that even a bad draughts-man working in the dark would be able to draw it better. If he had the power to change it, he would give less *relief* to some of its parts. This man has always been fairly satisfied with his health, although it is not of the best; he has to a high degree the gift of profiting from his good days. On such occasions his imagination, his most faithful companion, never deserts him; he stands behind the window, his head propped between his hands, and – while the passer-by sees nothing but a melancholically drooping head – he often silently confesses to himself that once again he has too much indulged in pleasure.

He has few friends; actually his heart is always open only to one friend who is present, but to several absent ones also. His friendliness makes many believe that he is their friend. He serves them out of ambition or humaneness, but in this he's not driven by that impulse which drives him to serve his real friends. He has loved only once or twice, once not unhappily, but the other time happily. He won, merely through gaiety and lightheartedness, a good soul, with the result that these now often fail him. Yet he will for ever revere gaiety and lightheartedness as those qualities of his soul which procured for him the most joyful hours of

9

his life : if he could choose a second life and another soul, I doubt whether he would choose different ones.

About religion he had very free thoughts already as a boy, but he never sought any special recognition for being a freethinker, nor for believing everything without exception. He can pray with fervour and has never been able to read the 90th psalm without an indescribable feeling of exaltation. He doesn't know which he hates more, young officers or young preachers; he wouldn't be able to live for long with either. His body and his attire have seldom been good enough for formal parties, and his convictions seldom ... * enough. He hopes he will never have meals of more than three courses at noon and two in the evening, with some wine, nor does he ever want to be reduced to less than potatoes, apples, bread and some wine every day. In either case he would be unhappy. Reading and writing are as necessary to him as eating and drinking, and he hopes he will never lack books. Of death he thinks often, and never with aversion; he wishes he could think of everything with the same detachment, and hopes that, when the time comes, his Creator will gently take from him a life of which he was, it is true, not a very economical, but neither a wicked owner.

I remember distinctly that, when I was quite young, I once wanted to teach a calf how to retrieve, yet although I saw at once that I was improving noticeably in the necessary skills, we understood one another less each day, and finally I gave up completely and have never tried again.

* Lichtenberg's dots.

(*Lion*)* Often finds pleasure in figuring out means of killing this or that person, or of setting fires without its being noticed. Without ever having firmly resolved to do such a thing, or having even the least inclination, he very often fell asleep thinking such thoughts. After his sixteenth year, he could no longer convince himself that Christ was God's son. This idea became so familiar to him and so much part of him that there was no more thought of trying to convince him. He regretted only that Christ Himself did not write and leave us more information about Joseph of Arimathea. He knew too well what pious fanatics can do in such a situation. His faith in the efficacy of prayer, his superstition in many respects – kneeling, touching the Bible and kissing it; downright adoration of his sainted mother.

(Lion). In his 10th year he falls in love with a boy callel Schmidt (the head boy in the town school), son of a tailor. Likes to hear anything about him and induces the boys to talk about their conversations with him; has never himself spoken to him, but was very pleased to hear that the boy had spoken about him. Climbed a wall after school to watch him go home from school. Now, still remembers his features very distinctly; the boy seems to him nothing less than handsome, with a turned-up nose and red cheeks. But he was at the head of his form. I would regret it if, by admitting this freely, I should increase distrust of the world, but I was a human being. Lion knew few people in the world whose weakness he hadn't found out after three weeks' acquaintance (counting the hours

* *Lion* (in English) indicates remarks about himself.

11

of association only, which could well amount to three months in the calendar) and he has become convinced that no dissembling helps against an association of three weeks. Has never acted unjustly from avarice, so help me God.

Desultory reading has always been my greatest pleasure.

I must not forget that I once put the question 'What are the Northern Lights?' addressed to an angel, on the floor of Graupner's attic, and next morning sneaked up there, most shyly, for the note. Oh, if only some practical joker had answered the note!

In the house where I lived, I had learned the sound and the pitch of each step of the old wooden stairs and also the time which each of my friends beat when he came to call on me. I must confess that I trembled every time I heard the stairs played upon by some pair of feet coming up in a melody unknown to me.

I know little about music and can't play any instrument – except that I can whistle well. I've derived more advantage from this than many others have from their arias on the flute and the harpsichord. I should try in vain to express in words what I feel when I whistle the hymn 'In all my earthly doings' really well on a quiet evening and *think* the words to it.

There are in our thoughts certain trade winds which at certain times blow constantly, and – we may steer and shift however we wish – they are always blown into the same direction. On such November days as the present ones, all my thoughts drift between melancholy and self-disparagement unless some special current drives me sideways, and often I would no longer be able to find myself if the two compasses, Friendship and Wine, did not direct me and give me courage to fight *against a sea of troubles*. Today my mind was following the thoughts of the great Newton through the universe, not without being tickled by a kind of pride : I am, therefore, made of the same substance after all as that great man, because I can understand his thoughts, and my brain has fibres which respond to those thoughts, and what God proclaimed to posterity through this man is heard by me, while it glides over the ears of millions, unperceived.

The play of imagination with which I follow the subtlest turn of a description by Wieland* and create my own world, through which I stroll like a magician, seeing the kernels of some slight frivolity blossom into vast fields of intellectual pleasure – this imagination is, in its most rapid flight, often attracted by a delicately curved nose, by an uncovered healthy arm, so forcefully that nothing remains of its previous motion but a fleeting tremor. And so I hang in the world suspended between philosophy and the cunning of housemaids, between the most spiritual vistas and the most sensual feelings and stagger from those into these until after a short struggle my twofold Self will come to rest some future time, and I shall, totally

* German poet of the eighteenth century, noted for his subtle, sensuous imagination.

divided, rot here and evaporate into a pure life there. We two, I and my body, have never before been *two* so much as now; sometimes we don't even recognize one another; then we run against each other in such a way that both of us don't know where we are.

How did you like it at this party? Answer: Just fine, almost as well as in my room by myself.

Many things hurt me which only annoy other people.

He can, before you say the Lord's Prayer, enumerate ten circumstances to be considered. Thoughts come to him as if a goblin were supplying them.

He kept on hand a little piece of paper on which he usually wrote whatever he regarded as a special demonstration of God's grace, and which could not possibly be explained in any other way. When praying most ardently he sometimes said: *Dear God, something to put on my little piece of paper!*

I cannot deny it: When I saw for the first time that people in my country began to know the meaning of the radical sign in mathematics, clear tears of joy came into my eyes.

P.m.* used to say I have surely been saved for some great crime, since I must overcome so many insults to my feelings that I have become indifferent to almost everything. If life didn't make a slight difference, it

* *P.m.* in Lichtenberg's diaries also means himself.

would be the same to me whether I were elevated at Tyburn* or at St. James's.

Noticed blindness on April 9th, 1775.

On the evening of April 15th, the Saturday before Easter, I went for a walk in Hyde Park after tea; it may have been a quarter of seven. The moon had just risen; it was full moon and it was shining from above Westminster Abbey. The solemnity of the eve of such a day made me indulge in my favourite meditations with voluptuous melancholy. I sauntered down Piccadilly and the Haymarket to Whitehall, partly in order to look again on the statue of Charles the First against the bright western sky, partly to give myself up in the moonlight to meditations in view of the Banqueting Hall, the house through the window of which Charles the First walked out on to the scaffold. It so happened that I saw there one of the men who hire organs from the organ-makers and play while walking through the streets, until someone calls them and for sixpence has them play through their pieces. Suddenly he began to play the beautiful chorale, 'In allen meinen Taten',† in such a melancholy way, so much in harmony with my mood at that time that a shudder of indescribable awe came over me. There, in the moonlight, under the open sky, I was thinking of my friends far away. My sorrows became endurable and vanished entirely. We had walked perhaps 200 steps beyond the famous

---

* In Lichtenberg's time, place of public execution in London. St James's: the king's palace there.
† 'In all my deeds', one of the best-known German church songs.

Banqueting Hall. I called the fellow, led him nearer to the house, and there I told him to play that magnificent hymn. While he was playing, I could not refrain from singing the words quietly to myself :

> 'Hast du es denn beschlossen,
> So will ich unverdrossen
> An mein Verhängnis gehn.'*

Before me lay the majestic building lit by the full moon. It was Easter Eve, the Mediator's death – here through this window Charles had stepped down to exchange the temporal crown for the eternal one. Oh God, what is the greatness of this world!

Something could have been made of his ideas if an angel had organized them for him.

Once the nerves have become so weak that it is impossible for a man to resolve to undertake steps towards his own recovery, he is lost.

Impressions are still alive in my mind made by causes which vanished a long time ago (my dear mother ! ! ! ! ! ! !).

I saw the grave on my cheeks, April 16th, 1777.

To believe that, in order to be liked by posterity, one has to be hated by one's contemporaries – this I was often on the point of believing with so much conviction that I felt an inclination to assail everything.

* 'If Thou has decided so, I shall meet my fate willingly.'

[A grave illness struck Lichtenberg in 1789. It had its origin in an organic ailment, yet his doctors and later medical experts who have read his notes have agreed that his relentless suffering during and after his illness must have been mainly of a neurotic nature. Diaries which have been published only recently bear this out. When, after one and a half years in bed, he tried to return to a more normal life, his personality had changed. Despite the brief feelings of inner peace and joy over his recovery, mirrored in *Amintor's Morning Prayer*, despite periods of new happiness with his wife and children, gaiety had gone from him. He lived the last decade of his life in an almost continuous state of depression and anxiety. Forty-eight years old, he suffered from the feeling that he was ageing rapidly; he felt lonely, but tried to keep strangers away from his home and never left it to visit friends or attend social affairs. Nothing could give him joy any longer but nature – carriage rides in the spring, the singing of the birds in the stillness of his garden outside the city gate – and recognition from the men whom he himself admired. The anxieties of the last five or six years of his life were increased by a secret amorous relationship which was more an affair of his senses than of his heart and which caused him more torment and feelings of guilt than happiness. The brilliance of his mind faded, but his wisdom became more indulgent. His self-observation went on as ever; a dozen notes, chosen from the many intended for his autobiography, allow us glimpses into his inner life at that time. F.M.]

E.g.: He was lying down because of abdominal

cramps; this was his only ailment according to the testimony of the best doctors. But the number of ailments he believed he had was considerable : 1) *marasmus senilis*, although he was only 46 years old; 2) incipient dropsy; 3) convulsive asthma; 4) slow fever; 5) jaundice; 6) hydrothorax; 7) he was afraid of a stroke; 8) paralysis of his right side; 9) he believed his big arteries and veins were sclerotic; 10) he had some growth in his heart; 11) a tumour on his liver; and 12) water in his head. A person reading this might almost believe the twelfth was the only fear which had some foundations. 13) diabetes.

During my nervous illness I very frequently found that what formerly hurt my moral sense, now also affected my body. When Dieterich* once said 'May God kill me', I felt so sick that I had to forbid him my room for some time.

Few people probably send books into the world without expecting that everyone will now put down his pipe or will light one in order to read them. I do not say only that I'm not destined for this honour – that would be easy – I also believe it, which is a little more difficult and has to be learned.

The worst thing about this illness is that I can no longer think or feel any thing without, at the same time, feeling mainly myself. I see the entire world as a machine which has the purpose of making me feel my sickness and my suffering in every possible way. A pathological egotist. Pusillanimity is the right word for

* Lichtenberg's publisher, landlord and life-long friend

my illness, but can one get rid of it? He who can overcome it would deserve an honorary column, but who will erect an honorary column for the person who transforms himself from an old woman into a man?

O God! if one could only keep always learning in this world, without being *observed*. What a heavenly pleasure the knowledge of the stars afforded me in youth. Thou God of justice! I know no fairer times; they were the happiest of my life. The envy and mockery of other people, who know a little more than I do about this or that point, is unbearable. How blissful my life was in those days! Now that everything I do is observed, and by many a person who's not worth half what I am and who opposes to my original endeavour some remark which he's simply learned by heart, they laugh in my face.

The night from Easter Sunday, 1792, to Easter Monday, I dreamed that I was going to be burned alive. I was very calm about it, which did not please me at all when I awoke. I had been reasoning very calmly about the length of time it would take. I'm almost afraid everything in me becomes thought, and feeling vanishes.

I used to get angry with a feeling of vigour, but now it is with a feeling of passive timidity.

He had even framed a constitution in order to force himself to act, and appointed real ministers – Temperance, once even Avarice. But they were overthrown again and again.

That I always compare the years of an author whose Life I am reading, with my own – something I did even in my youth – is entirely within human nature.

It was a great mistake in my youthful studies that I made the design for the building too great. The result was that I could not finish the upper storey, indeed could not even put on the roof. In the end I found myself forced to be content with a few little rooms in the attic which I finished pretty well, but I could not keep out the rain in bad weather. Many others have the same experience!

Trembling, when we are getting weak, could almost make one believe that our will affects our body in a succession of jerks, and that the continuity in our movements has the same relationship to trembling as has a curved line to a polygon (I understand myself). One can be witty at any age, I believe, only it does not proceed in such a steady flow as when we are young. (One trembles then, too.) If we collect the remarks and take out the intervals, then the reader won't be able to notice the decline of strength.

Frequently I have indulged in all sorts of fantasies, and this at times when people thought I was very busy. I realized how harmful this was with regard to loss of time, but without this fantasy treatment – which I usually underwent with eagerness at the season for taking the waters – I should not have reached my present age, 53 years and $1\frac{1}{2}$ months.

Formerly when I fished in my mind for thoughts or

ideas I always caught something; now the fish no longer come so readily. They're starting to petrify on the bottom, and I have to chop them loose. At times I only get them out in pieces and patch them together.

He had names for his two slippers.

APHORISMS

It is hard to state how we arrived at the ideas we now hold. No one, or very few persons, can state when they first heard the name of Leibniz. It would be still harder to state when we first arrived at the idea that all men must die; we do not acquire it as quickly as people generally believe. Hard as it is to state the origin of phenomena which transpire within us, how will it be when we want to make such a statement with reference to things exterior to us?

The asses perhaps owe the sad situation in which they now live in the world only to the witticism of a wag. It is his fault that they have become, and will remain for ever, the despised animal, for many donkey-drivers treat their wards so terribly because they are asses, not because they are lazy and slow.

Many conclusions about men's characters could perhaps be drawn from their dreams, if they would report them exactly. But quite a few would be needed, not just one.

Violent ambition and suspicion I have always seen going hand in hand.

We often strive to subdue some vicious emotion, and try at the same time to preserve all of our good ones. This comes from our method of describing man : we fail to see his character as a very neatly constructed totality, which can be rearranged only by changing the relative position of its various parts. Rather, we regard his emotions as adhesive beauty-patches, which we may shift or throw away at will. Many such errors derive from the languages indispensable in describing the emotions. Thus we always think of the most ordinary meaning the moment we neglect, to the slightest degree, the particular association. Therefore, if a general system of characterization is to be invented, a proper language must first be found.

I should like to know on every evening that second of the past day when my life had the least value, when – if purity of intention and safety of life had a cash value – I would have been worth least.

The critics instruct us to stay close to nature, and authors read this advice; but they always think it safer to stay close to authors who have stayed close to nature.

If we could express ourselves as completely as we feel, talkers would find few refractory listeners; and lovers, few cruel ladies. Our whole body wishes, when a beloved girl is about to depart, that she would stay; no organ can convey this as clearly as the mouth, but how is it to convey its message in such a way that the wishes of the other organs are also perceived to some extent?

There is a certain sort of people who easily make friends with everyone, just as quickly hate him, and then love him again. If one thinks of the human race as a whole, in which each part fits in its place, such people are 'fillers', to be inserted anywhere. One seldom finds men of genius among people of this sort, though they are very easily taken for geniuses.

Everyone admits that the dirty stories we make up ourselves have a far less dangerous effect on us than other people's do.

We are ourselves the measure of the miraculous; if we should find a universal measure, the miraculous element would disappear, and all things would be of equal size.

Man's happiness consists of a proper relationship of his traits of character to his emotions; if one trait grows stronger, all the others suffer, and countless combinations result. What we call a 'great mind' may just as well be a monstrosity, as a gambler is; but it is a useful monstrosity.

The man who lives calmly and cheerfully is the true human being. Such a man will rarely make very great progress in any field, for a machine which has many functions can rarely perform each of them as usefully as one designed only for a single purpose Therefore, the wisdom of Providence is as much revealed in the rarity of genius, as in the circumstance that not everyone is deaf or blind.

All languages have the inescapable defect that they express only the *genera* of concepts and seldom can adequately say what they intend to say. For if we compare our words with things, we discover that the latter are arrayed in quite a different order from the former. The qualities we observe in our souls are connected in such a way that it is not easy to establish a boundary between any two of them, but the words by which we express them are not thus constituted; and two successive, related qualities are expressed by signs which do not reflect this relationship. One ought to be able to decline words philosophically, i.e., to state their relationships under a given aspect by making the appropriate changes. In the geometrical analysis of a line a, one indefinite section of it is called x; the other section is not y, as it would be in ordinary life, but $a - x$. This is the reason that mathematical language has such great advantages over ordinary speech.

There is no doubt that creatures may exist whose organs are so delicate that they are unable to reach through a ray of light, just as we are unable to reach through a stone because our hands would be destroyed first.

Perhaps a thought is the cause of all motion in the world, and the philosophers who have taught that the world is an animal may have hit upon the notion in this way : they may have failed only to express themselves as exactly as they ought perhaps to have done. Our whole world is only the effect upon matter of one of God's thoughts.

Not to exist means to natural scientists – at least to those of a certain type – the same as not to be perceived.

Why is it that we are able at times resolutely to banish a secret sorrow – since the idea that we are protected by a most benevolent Providence affects us so strongly – and yet we almost succumb, within the next half-hour, to this same sorrow? That's the way things are with me, at least. But I couldn't say that I regard my sorrow from a different point of view the second time, or see it in a different context – by no means. If this were what took place, I would not even have jotted down this observation. Rather, I believe that the moral sensitivity of man is different at various times, stronger in the morning than in the evening.

To become wiser means to become increasingly acquainted with the errors to which this instrument with which we perceive and judge can be subject. Today the thing to be recommended to each and every one is caution in making judgments. If we could obtain only one indisputable truth every ten years from each philosophically inclined author, our harvest would still be rich enough.

A landscape can easily be composed of a number of haphazard strokes, but not a piece of music of haphazard sounds.

When he was expected to use his mind, he felt like a right-handed person who has to do something with his left.

The ordinary man is ruined by the flesh lusting against the spirit; the scholar by the spirit lusting too much against the flesh.

Everyone should study at least enough philosophy and *belles lettres* to make his sexual experience more delectable.

I have observed that persons whose faces are somewhat asymmetrical often possess the subtlest minds.

Every man has his moral backside too, which he doesn't expose unnecessarily but keeps covered as long as possible by the trousers of decorum.

At the comedy, whenever something seemed ridiculous to him, he looked around for someone to laugh with him. When I noticed this, I never came to his aid but looked steadily away.

What I mean by 'moral ether' is really that spiritual element present in all our actions, even the smallest, and flowing through all of them; it is to be found in 'and he took a pinch of snuff' as much as in Corneille's 'Qu'il mourût' or his tight-packed 'Soyons amis, Cinna'.

In woman the seat of the *point d'honneur* coincides with the centre of gravity; in man it is located rather higher, in the chest, near the diaphragm. Thence, in man, the buoyant fullness in that region when he embarks on splendid deeds, and thence too the flabby emptiness there when he embarks on petty ones.

Undeniably, what we call perseverance can lend the appearance of dignity and grandeur to many actions, just as silence in company affords wisdom and apparent intelligence to a stupid person.

It was a rash action, but I did it with that warmth without which my life would mean far less to me than it does now. Finally I went to bed, bitterly reproaching myself, with the feeling that I had lost a good bit of moral poundage.

Her petticoat had very wide red and blue stripes and looked as if it were made of theatre curtain. I'd have paid a lot for a front-row-centre seat, but the curtain was never raised.

Wit and humour, like all corrosives, must be used with care.

If an angel were to tell us about his philosophy, I believe many of his statements might well sound like '$2 \times 2 = 13$'.

Look out, or your slowness will make my patience run down. On my honour, I shan't wind it up again for your sake.

Whenever we change, a lot of things get too big or too small for us; useless, in a word. Just as we outgrow a pair of trousers, we outgrow acquaintances, libraries, principles, etc., at times before they're worn out and at times – and this is the worst of all – before we have new ones.

He moved as slowly as an hour-hand amidst a crowd of second-hands.

It would not be good if suicides could frequently tell their reasons in the language of absolute truth. As it is, every listener reduces them for himself into his own language; in this way he does not just weaken them : he changes them into something entirely different. In order to understand a person completely, one would sometimes have to be that person. Whoever understands what a personal system of thought is, will subscribe to this. To be alone frequently and to think about ourselves and to create our world out of ourselves, may give us great joy; but in this way we work, without noticing it, towards a philosophy according to which suicide is only right and permissible. It is good, therefore, to hook oneself to the world by means of a girl or a friend, in order not to fall off completely.

A certain friend of mine used to divide his body into three floors – his head, his chest and his abdomen. He often wished that the tenants of the top floor and those of the bottom would get along with each other better.

Now your hand, my dear ... Your mouth ... So, more next time. So long.

To give great pleasure to a beloved person even by our own pleasure is the most charming thing that a sensitive being can imagine. This is why gracious Nature has promised this premium to the person who would take the trouble of making others resembling himself.

We must make people feel obliged to us in accordance with what they are, not we.

1772–5

The pleasures of imagination are, so to speak, nothing but sketches with which the poor people play who cannot buy the other pleasures.

I saw once in Stade such peacefulness combined with a furtive smile – in the face of a fellow who had succeeded in driving his swine into a bathing place which they usually disliked entering – as I have never seen since.

I actually noticed on his face that mist which usually rises during our feeling of bliss when we believe ourselves superior to others.

Not greatness of the mind but of the wind has made him the man he is.

He does not have the gallows on his back, but in his eyes.

Teach me how to give strength to my salutary intentions; teach me to will with earnestness what I will; teach me steadfastness where the storms of destiny or an uncovered white arm make tremble the structure that it has taken me three years to build. Teach me to talk to the hearts of men so that my words will not be deflected in the refractory medium of their systems of convictions. Add the genius of Horace, and your glory shall resound throughout the ages.

In this expression the thought has too much play; I pointed with the head of a cane where I should have pointed with the tip of a needle.

A king gives orders that under penalty of death people shall believe a stone to be a diamond.

Just as foolish as it must look to a crab when it sees a man walk forward.

A grave is still the best fortification against the storms of destiny.

He pondered things over so meticulously; he always saw a grain of sand before he saw a house.

With voluptuous anxiety.

There is a great difference between *still* believing

something and believing it *again*. *Still* to believe that the moon affects the plants reveals stupidity and superstition, but to believe it *again* is a sign of philosophy and reflection.

Nothing can contribute more to peace of soul than having no opinion at all.

Whoever has two pairs of pants, sell one and buy this book.

If someone writes badly – very well, let him write! To make an ass of oneself is a long way from suicide.

Courage, chattering and the crowd are on our side. What more do we want?

What is a 'German character'? What? Tobacco-smoking and honesty, didn't you say? O you simple dolts! Listen: be good enough to tell me what the weather is like in America. Shall I tell instead of you? All right. It lightens, it hails, it's muddy, it's sultry, it's unbearable, it's snowing, freezing, windy and the sun is shining.

The heathen Tacitus, whose eye penetrated, with Jewish subtlety, down to the devil at the bottom of every action.

They sell everything down to the last shirt – and beyond.

One sip of reason.

Such people ought to be made to wear badges marked with the number Zero, so one could recognize them.

It's incredible how much our best words have lost. The word *reasonable* has lost almost all its character; people know the meaning but don't feel it any more because of the mass of 'reasonable' men who have borne this epithet. *Unreasonable* is stronger in its way. A reasonable child is a slack, pious, no-good tattle-tale; an unreasonable boy is much better.

There are people who think that everything one does with a serious face is sensible.

In a little town where each face rhymes with every other.

For shame! To quarrel over such trifles is to set up batteries to shoot at thrushes; reasonable people scarcely know whether you dealt the blow or received it.

The paths are bordered with nevergreen.

Now, after we've got to know Nature thoroughly, even a child will see that an experiment is nothing more than a compliment we pay her. It is a mere ceremony: we know in advance what her answer will be. We ask Nature for her consent as great lords ask their Provincial Estates.

Yes, I too like to admire great men, but only those whose works I do not understand.

Because of his obscure sense of his own perfectibility, man still thinks himself far from the goal even when he has reached it; and reason does not sufficiently enlighten him. What he finds easy, he thinks bad, and so he strains from the bad to the good, and from the good to a type of the bad which he thinks better than good.

The progress of the good and the purposeful in the world. If, for instance, it is rooted in human nature that ultimately the Christian religion will perish again some day, it will happen whether people oppose this or not. Going against the stream and obstructing it for a little while makes only an infinitely small bend in the line. Only it is too bad that *we* have to be the spectators and not some other generation; no one can blame us for working as hard as we can to shape our times according to our own minds.

I always think that we on this sphere serve a purpose whose fulfilment a conspiracy of the whole human race cannot prevent. In just the same way a good book will go down to posterity even if all the critical judges should combine to cast suspicion on it – not by satire but with the mien of the innocent lamb and the accent of the lover of truth – even if they should keep absolute silence about it. If it contains a dozen new truths, stated well and vigorously, if the expert in human nature appears in the rest of the work, then a legion of witty magazine writers will be as little able to block its course to eternity as I could fan back the storm or the rising flood with a playing card. A man can condemn a good book through envy, lack of judgment or foolishness, but Man cannot.

The secret of the ridiculous is probably Möser's* *bigness without strength*. Strength without bigness is never laughable, but bigness without strength almost always.

We should not separate too much, not abstract too much : the great *raffineurs* have made the fewest discoveries, I believe. The usefulness of the human machine is precisely that it shows totals.

The enthusiasts whom I have known all had the dreadful fault that, at the least spark which fell upon them, they always went up in flames like fireworks prepared long in advance – always in the same manner and always with the same uproar – whereas the feeling of a reasonable man is always proportionate to the impression. The frivolous man keeps cold-bloodedly on arguing after his first impression, while the reasonable man turns round now and then to see what instinct has to say.

We acquire professors, promising young people; we acquire books, read, excerpt and argue ourselves white, yellow, consumptive – and frigid and impotent.

People who have read a great deal seldom make great discoveries. I don't say this as an excuse for lazi-

* Justus Möser : contemporary historian and critic.

ness, for inventing presupposes a far-reaching, original observation of things: one must see rather than be a listener. Association.

I don't use the word *devil*, which frequently occurs in my little work, in the sense in which the common people take it, but like recent philosophers, in order to keep peace with all sects. Thus it is rather to be compared with the *x, y, z* of the algebraists, an unknown quantity.

What sort of an effect must it have on a people not to learn any foreign languages? Presumably an effect rather similar to that which a complete withdrawal from all society has on an individual.

Educating the mothers means training the children in the womb.

There is no surer way to make oneself a name than by writing about things which have a semblance of importance but which a reasonable man is not likely to take the time to investigate for himself.

1775–9

There's no surer criterion of a great writer than that books can be made, *en passant*, out of his incidental remarks. Tacitus and Sterne are models of this, each in his own way.

To do just the opposite is also a form of imitation, and the definitions of imitation ought by rights to include both.

To read means to borrow; to create out of one's readings is paying off one's debts.

As soon as a man begins to see everything in everything, he generally expresses himself obscurely – begins to speak with the tongue of angels.

To make astute people believe that one is what one is not, is harder in most cases than actually to become what one wants to appear.

We, the tail of the world, don't know what the head is planning.

It rained so hard that all the pigs got clean and all the people dirty.

In courteous towns it is impossible to acquire any knowledge of the world; everyone is so courteously honest, so courteously rude, so courteously deceitful that a man can seldom get angry enough to write a satire. These people always deserve compassion. In a word, everything lacks strength.

The writer who can't at times throw away a thought about which another would have written dissertations, unworried whether or not the reader will find it, will never become a great writer.

A book is a mirror: when a monkey looks in, no apostle can look out.

Where people know man only from books and see in all matters only what they already know.

I have already observed elsewhere that everything in the world is diffused into everything and everything is to be found in everything. I mean that everything which we observe and designate with a particular word was already there before it reached the degree which we could observe. The example of the storm : all clouds are one, and can be distinguished only in degree.

Why is it that disagreeable thoughts pain us much more keenly in the morning, when we awaken, than some time later, when we know that everyone is awake; or when we have risen; or in the middle of the day; or also when we are lying in bed in the evening? I have had abundant experience of this : I have gone to bed quite reassured about certain matters about which I was again greatly troubled around 4 in the morning, so that I often lay awake and tossed for several hours. By 9 o'clock, or even earlier, indifference or hope had returned.

In our times, when insects collect insects and butterflies prattle of butterflies.

To think highly of a matter, people must not see it complete; rather, a part must be hidden for conjecture. Thus in most cases we have a lower opinion of a man after his tenth book than before his first, not because he has written himself out, but because by then we have enough points known to draw his whole lifeline. Everywhere a well-displayed supply is more pleasing than extravagance.

At the end of a complicated syllogism one can consult common sense in about the way that the mathematician makes sure, by a geometrical construction or even a rougher estimate, that he has not made a mistake. If the estimate contradicts the calculation, he calculates again to see in which of the two the error lies.

He has been so long at giving birth without anything coming of it that even now presumably nothing will come of it unless there's a Caesarean operation.

He was a busy writer and a very diligent reader of his own articles in the learned periodicals.

What they call 'heart' is located far lower than the fourth waistcoat button.

That was way back when time still had no beard.

If a later generation were to reconstruct the man of today from our sentimental writings, they would believe he had been a heart with testicles.

The metaphor is far more intelligent than its author, and this is the case with many things. Everything has its depths. He who has eyes sees something in everything.

The Greeks possessed a knowledge of mankind which we apparently can hardly attain without going through the invigorating hibernation of a new barbarism.

To live in fratrimony.

In an ordinance one could decree the sacrifice of verse firstlings.

How close may our thoughts come at times to grazing on a great discovery?

Just as one says someone 'holds an office', while actually the office holds him.

Doubt must be nothing more than vigilance, otherwise it can become dangerous.

I am convinced that a person doesn't only love himself in others; he also hates himself in others.

Man becomes a sophist and super-subtle in fields where he has no adequate store of solid information.

Materialism is the asymptote of psychology.

An alert thinker will often find more that is instructive and delightful in the playful writings of great men than in their serious works. The formal, conventional, ceremonial is usually omitted from them; it is amazing how much wretched conventional stuff still appears in

43

our way of narrating in print. Most writers put on airs, just like many people when they are having their portraits painted.

About the peculiar charm of white paper, bound into a book. Paper which hasn't yet lost its virginity and still shines in the colour of innocence is always better than after it has been used.

I cannot say that I was his enemy, but neither was I his friend; I have never dreamed of him.

It is difficult to feel the monkey-ishness in the human foot, but sometimes I can; then one discovers easily what is human and conventional.

An intelligent child who is brought up with a mad child can go mad. Man is so perfectible and corruptible that he can become a madman through sheer intellect.

If it is true, as I once read, that no one dies before he has done at least one sensible thing, then M——— has begotten an immortal son.

The girl is quite all right; one only has to put another frame around her.

We must not believe, when we make a few discoveries in this field or that, that this process will just keep going on for ever. The high-jumper jumps higher than the ploughboy, and one high-jumper better than another, but the height which no human can jump over is very small. Just as people find water whenever they dig, man everywhere finds the incomprehensible, sooner or later.

There is a sort of transcendental ventriloquy through which men can be made to believe that something which was said on earth came from heaven.

A philosophical dream book could be written. People have made the *interpretations of dreams* bear the brunt of their precocious zeal, which actually should have been turned only against *dream books*. That's the way it usually is. I know from undeniable experience that dreams lead to self-knowledge.

Just as there are mechanics of genius who do splendid work with a few inferior instruments, there are also people who know how to use their slight learning and to extend their experiences so widely that a so-called scholar can hardly rival them.

I commend dreams again; we live and feel as much dreaming as waking and are the one as much as the other. It is one of the superiorities of man that he dreams *and knows it*. We have hardly made the right use of this yet. Dream is a life which, combined with the rest of us, makes up what we call human life. Dreams gradually merge into our waking; we cannot say where man's waking state begins.

All the shallow great writers of our time.

Where affectation begins to be one's true nature.

One of the main conveniences of marriage is to be able to pass a visitor whom one can't stand along to one's wife.

God creates the animals; man creates himself.

For the time being, one must not make the world believe that what we seek can really be found or, worse, has been found. Especially if one has some authority.

People don't like to choose lot #1 in a lottery. 'Choose it,' Reason cries loudly. 'It has as good a chance of winning the 12,000 thalers as any other.' 'In Heaven's name don't choose it,' a *je ne sais quoi* whispers. 'There's no example of such little numbers being listed before great winnings.' And actually no one takes it.

The sounds of the nations are innumerable, and the Englishman has his *th* in all his deeds. One can't imitate his deeds any more than his speech.

A healthy appetite and the high regard for women which is usually combined with it.

A man construes all the vague sarcasms he hears as references to himself and thinks people had him secretly in mind.

The most successful and therefore the most dangerous seducers are the 'deluded deluders'.

A great strength of feeling, of which so many boast, is all too often the result of a decay of the intellectual powers. I am not very hard-hearted, but the compassion I often feel in my dreams is incomparably greater than when my brain is awake; the former is a pleasure which closely approaches pain.

Oh, I know all too well the people who, because of humbled pride or blind ardour, always nest a mile above or below the truth.

Whenever the sophisticated men of the world say 'God knows why', it is always a sure indication that, in addition to God, they know an important man who also knows.

Our sensibility is certainly *not* the measure of the beauty of the vast plan of nature.

An ass had the task of carrying the statue of Isis, and when the populace honoured the statue by falling down before it, he thought the honour had been paid to him.

People who have taken no intellectual food for ten years, except a few tiny crumbs from the journals, are found even among professors; they aren't rare at all.

This is a very fertile truth: if kept in a sound brain

it has, like the coins in Fortunatus' purse, a new one lying beside it every morning.

I can't deny that my distrust of the taste of our time has perhaps risen in me to a reprehensible height. To see every day how people get the name 'genius' just as the wood-lice in the cellar the name 'millipede' – not because they have that many feet, but because most people don't want to count to 14 – this has had the result that I don't believe anyone any more without checking.

How odd it would be if a man's mouth should some day begin to tell his most secret affairs without his being able to stop it; and during all this, he would have to keep complete command of his intelligence.

Not at all is really a phrase suitable only for angels; *very little* is more for men.

It is well known that the man belongs to the class of the so-called pompous writers who find 'lovely' only everything gorgeously fake. Thus the author of the *Letter* says that Versailles compared to Sans Souci had seemed to him like the dwelling of a dwarf contrasted to that of a giant. Now not one word of that is true, nor did it really seem like that to him; but it seemed to him at home that it *had* seemed that way; or it seemed to him that it would be lovely *if* it did seem like that; or, finally, it seemed to him it would be lovely just to *say* it had seemed so to him.

Actually there were only two persons in the world

whom he loved warmly: one was, at any given moment, his grossest flatterer, and the other was himself.

He loved pepper and zig-zag lines.

What makes a prolific author is often not his great knowledge but rather that fortunate relation between his abilities and his taste, by virtue of which the latter always approves what the former have produced.

I would often rather read what a famous author has cut from one of his works than what he has let stand.

His inkwell was a veritable temple of Janus; when it was corked up, there was peace in all the world.

Some actions are called malicious because they're done by ugly people.

God, who winds our sundials.

First there is a time when we believe everything without reasons. Then, for a short time, we believe discriminatingly. Then we believe nothing at all. And then we believe everything again and, indeed, cite reasons why we believe everything.

They feel with their heads and think with their hearts.

The impulse to propagate our race has propagated a lot of other things too.

By reading so much we have contracted a sort of learned barbarism.

Indisputably, masculine beauty has not yet been portrayed enough by those hands which alone could do so – feminine hands.

At the ball, when the company went out to supper, it had settled around a couple of girls like filings around a magnet.

While we don't burn witches any more, we do burn every letter which contains a blunt truth.

A physical experiment which makes a bang is always worth more than a quiet one. Therefore a man cannot strongly enough ask of Heaven: if It wants to let him discover something, may it be something that makes a bang. It will resound into eternity.

As soon as people know that someone is blind, they think they can tell it from behind.

Often, when an acquaintance passes by, I leave the window – not so much to save him the trouble of bowing, as rather to save myself the embarrassment of seeing that he doesn't bow.

Seeing ourselves in dreams comes from seeing ourselves in the mirror at times without thinking that it *is* in the mirror. But in dreams the image is more vivid, and conscious thinking is slighter.

There actually is a sort of reserved and sensitive people who look, when they are happy, like others when they weep.

Where major issues are concerned, I have carefully refrained from anything which my opponents might call inspirations of wit. For anyone who has such inspirations finds it easy, if he sticks rather firmly to his intention, to avoid the consequences of being witty; while usually those who reproach him for it would not themselves have refrained unless forced to by incurable impotence.

I can quite easily imagine how easily praise in the newspapers can seduce a man into believing that he finally is what these people claim for him.

To me, it's a very unpleasant feeling when someone feels pity for me, in the usual sense of the word. Similarly, when people are really angry at someone, they use the expression, 'One has to pity a person like that.' This sort of pity is a giving of alms, and alms presuppose need on the one side and abundance on the other, however insignificant it may be. But there is a much less selfish sort of pity which is genuinely concerned, which moves quickly to act and to save, and is seldom accompanied by sentimental melancholizing (*sit venia verbo*).* One could call the former 'alms-giving pity' and the latter 'pity as an offensive and defensive alliance'.

The scribble-book method is most warmly to be

* 'May I be forgiven for this expression.'

recommended. To leave no idiom, no expression unwritten. We can acquire riches by saving up the penny truths, too.

At times we admire the energy of the languages of uncultivated peoples. Ours is no less energetic; our most everyday expressions are often very poetic. Yet the poetic aspect of an expression vanishes when it becomes commonplace; the *sound* then produces the concept, and the *image*, which previously was the medium, disappears and with it all the associated ideas.

1779–88

One man begets the thought, the second baptizes it, the third sires children on it, the fourth visits it on its deathbed and the fifth buries it.

Nowadays beautiful women are counted among the talents of their husbands.

It is delightful to hear a foreign woman speak our language and to hear lovely lips make mistakes. This is not the case with men.

The intelligent free-thinkers are a light flying column, always in the van, always reconnoitring the territory which the solemn corps of the orthodox, with its serried ranks, will also reach after all.

A girl, 150 books, a few friends and a view about four miles in diameter, were his world.

We don't devour each other; we merely slaughter each other.

Oh, how often I have confessed during the night in the hope that she would absolve me, and she has not absolved me!

I and *me*. *I* feel *me* – that makes two objects. Our false philosophy is embodied in the language as a whole: one might say that we can't reason without reasoning wrong. People don't bear in mind that speaking, no matter about what, is a philosophy. Everyone who speaks is a folk-philosopher, and our academic philosophy consists of qualifications of the popular brand. All our philosophy is an improving of linguistic usage; that is, an improving of a philosophy – of the most common of all, in fact. But the ordinary philosophy has the advantage of possessing declensions and conjugations. Thus we always teach true philosophy in the language of the false one. Defining words is no help; for by using explanations, I don't change the pronouns and their declensions.

How many ideas hover dispersed in my head of which many a pair, if they should come together, could bring about the greatest of discoveries! But they lie as far apart as Goslar sulphur from East India saltpetre, and both from the dust in the charcoal piles on the Eichsfeld – which three together would make gunpowder. How long the ingredients of gunpowder existed before gunpowder did! There is no natural *aqua regia*. If, when thinking, we yield too freely to the natural combinations of the forms of understanding and of reason, then our concepts often *stick* so much to others that they can't unite with those to which they really belong. If only there were something in that realm like a solution in chemistry, where the individual parts float about, lightly suspended, and thus can follow any current. But since this isn't possible, we must deliberately bring things into contact with each other. We must *experiment* with ideas.

The words *divine service* should be reassigned and no longer used for attending church, but only for good deeds.

As long as we don't really describe our lives, recording all our weaknesses, from those springing from ambition to the lowest vice, we shall never learn to love each other. [But if we attempt it,] complete equality, I hope, will be the result. The more it goes against the grain, the more truthful one must be towards oneself.

A man who has once stolen his hundred thousand dollars can live honestly ever after.

He swallowed a lot of wisdom, but it seemed as if all of it had gone down the wrong way.

A donkey appears to me like a horse translated into Dutch.

He was running a little business in obscurantism.

Everyone is a genius at least once a year. The real geniuses simply have their bright ideas closer together.

Now people are trying to spread wisdom everywhere; who knows whether, in a few hundred years, there won't be universities to restore ancient ignorance.

My hypochondria is really a proficiency in sucking out of every incident of life, whatever it may be, the greatest possible quantity of poison for my own use.

He who is in love with himself has at least this advantage: he won't encounter many rivals in his love.

How happily many people would live if they concerned themselves as little about others' affairs as about their own.

Some people display a talent for pretending to be silly, even before they become intelligent. Girls have this talent very often.

There is something in every person's character that cannot be broken – the bony structure of his character. Wanting to change it is the same as teaching a sheep to retrieve.

He can't hold his ink; and when he feels a desire to befoul someone, he usually befouls himself most.

'Age (the number of years) makes one astute' – that's true, but this doesn't mean any more than 'experience makes one astute'. On the other hand, 'Astuteness makes one *old*' (that is, remorse, ambition, *chagrin* make the cheeks sink in, the hair turn grey or fall out) is no less true. These daily lessons driven home by chastisement, not on the backside but on more dangerous parts, are a veritable poison.

The weakest of all men is the voluptuary – he who lusts after the body or the spirit. I mean the whoremonger or the god-hopper: the one who whores with girls, or the other who whores with religion.

The very fact that so many writers go out of their way to point out Frederick the Great's human weaknesses shows more clearly than all the praise of his panegyrists that they regard him as something superhuman. It's not so much that they try to humble him with their fault-finding as that they try to put him on a par with what we call a merely great man.

The highest point to which a weak but experienced mind can rise is skill in detecting the weaknesses of better men.

'Alas!' he cried when the accident occurred, 'if I'd only done something pleasantly wicked this morning, I'd at least know why I'm suffering now!'

First the book must be threshed out.

Even though walking on two legs isn't natural for man, it's certainly an invention which does him credit.

The myths of the physicists.

Overwiseness is one of the most contemptible kinds of unwiseness.

How did people ever arrive at the notion of freedom? It *was* a great thought.

Our theologians are trying by force to make the Bible into a book without common sense.

The room was quite empty except for a bit of secondhand sunshine which lay on the floor.

This whole theory is good for nothing except disputing about.

Non cogitant, ergo non sunt.

The fly that doesn't want to be swatted is most secure when it lights on the fly-swatter.

His beatings showed a sort of sex drive: he beat only his wife.

A fish which had drowned in the air.

Just as the supporters of Herr Kant always reproach their opponents for not understanding him, it seems

57

that some others believe that Herr Kant is right *because* they understand him.

I made the journey to knowledge like dogs who go for walks with their masters, a hundred times forward and backward over the same territory; and when I arrived I was tired.

Health is infectious.

A man can really never know whether he isn't sitting in a madhouse.

After a Thirty Years' War with himself, a compromise peace was made; but the time had been lost.

I am always grieved when a man of real talent dies, for the world needs such men more than Heaven does.

He could split a thought which everyone considered simple into seven others, as a prism splits sunlight; and each one of them always surpassed the one before. And then, another time he could collect a number of thoughts and produce the whiteness of sunlight, where others saw nothing but motley confusion.

It's questionable whether, when we break a murderer on the wheel we aren't lapsing into precisely the mistake of the child who hits the chair he bumps into.

One can live in this world on soothsaying, but not on truthsaying.

The ponderously learned bear, Dr Johnson.

In free France, where people are now free to string up anyone they want to.

With all my easy-going ways, I've always grown in self-knowledge without having the power to improve myself. Indeed, I've often considered myself indemnified for my indolence by the fact that I realized it; and my pleasure in precisely observing one of my weaknesses was often stronger than the annoyance provoked in me by my weakness itself. To me the professor was that much more important than the human being. Heaven guides its saints in strange ways.

A golden rule: one must judge men not by their opinions, but by what their opinions have made of them.

Condemning people hastily is due mainly to man's instinctive laziness.

Instead of saying that the world is mirrored in us, we should rather say that our reason is mirrored in the world. We can do no other than to descry order and wise government in the world, but this follows from the structure of our minds. But it does *not* follow that something which we must necessarily think, is really so, for we have no concept whatever of the true character of the external world. Thus no proof of the existence of God is possible on this basis alone.

A worry-meter, *mensura curarum*. My face is one

There are many people who won't listen until their ears are cut off.

That's another one of those fellows who believe that man is all finished and the Day of Judgment might as well begin now.

Completely to block a given effect requires a force equal to that which caused it. To give it a different direction, a trifle will often suffice.

In this town a certain happy dullness of intellect has always been endemic.

My body is that part of the world which my thoughts can change. Even *imaginary* illnesses can become real ones. In the rest of the world, my hypotheses cannot change the order of things.

They sense government pressure as little as they do air pressure.

Everything is good, so to speak, just as a plain strewn with grains of sand contains all possible kinds of patterns; one simply would have to mark the one which is most convenient. However, since one of them is certainly the best, we must create artificial motives. Religion and the philosopher create themselves the best ones. I regard every religion as an artificial system of motives to which authority has given the prestige – partly for subjective, partly for objective reasons – it might otherwise lack. The thing which won't move unless it's pushed must at least be pushed according to the rules.

Man is a masterpiece of creation, if for no other reason than this: despite all determinism, he believes that he acts as a free agent.

Always to search for final causes, not so much for their own sake as to discover how matters are inter-related, and as a purely heuristic device.

The more experiences and experiments accumulate in the exploration of nature, the more precarious the theories become. But it is not always good to discard them immediately on this account. For every hypo-thesis which once was sound was useful for thinking of previous phenomena in the proper interrelations and for keeping them in context. We ought to set down contradictory experiences separately, until enough have accumulated to make building a new structure worthwhile.

In your judgment, what is probably the worst, and what the finest deed you have done in your life? A question for one's own privy council.

To see something new, we must make something new.

It's certainly very characteristic of the German to arrange a few experiences in a system as soon as he has them; the Englishman doesn't act this way. Nothing hampers the advance of science more, as Bacon and a hundred others have already said.

What a chattering there would be in the world if people were determined to change the names of things to definitions.

Man is a creature who searches for causes; he could be named the cause-searcher within the hierarchy of minds. Other minds perhaps conceive things under other categories, incomprehensible to us.

Before anything else, extension of the frontiers of learning. Without this, all is in vain.

Philosophy is always the art of analysis, look at things as you will. The peasant uses all the propositions of the most abstract philosophy, only enveloped, hidden, tied down, latent, as the physicist and the chemist say. The philosopher gives us the propositions pure.

In nature we see not words but always the initial letters of words only, and if we then try to read, we discover that the new so-called words are again only the initials of others.

1793–9

The immeasurable benefit which language bestows on thought consists, I think, in the fact that words are generally signs for things rather than definitions What things are – to find that out is the task of philosophy. The word is intended to be, not a definition, but a mere sign for the definition, which in turn is always the variable result of the collective industriousness of scholars.

So be cautious about discarding words which are generally understood, and do not discard them if your only reason is that they might convey a false concept of the thing! In the first place, it is not true that a word conveys a false concept, because I indeed know and presuppose that it serves to distinguish the thing; and second, I don't claim to get to know the essence of the thing from the word.

Comparison between philosophy and hairdressing: both depend on fashion. Old wigs and old philosophy; the old professors of philosophy creep around, too, like old wig-makers.

The French Revolution, through the general idiom which it has brought about, has spread among the people a certain fund of knowledge which won't easily be destroyed. Who knows whether the great won't be compelled to institute barbarism?

A: You're twice as fat as before. B: That is the doing of exhausted nature, which no longer has the power to make anything except *fat*, which, if need be, one can cut away without offending the human condition. Fat, fat is neither spirit nor body, but only what weary nature leaves behind, valuable to me as to the grass in the churchyard. (Written at twilight)

Just let governments of the people take over everywhere; then presumably other conditions will ensue as unpalatable to Reason as the present ones. For that the republican system should be quite free of all harm is a dream, a mere notion. What would it be like if it should become reality? I believe, without wanting to set myself up as a judge, that society will be hurled by revolutions for ever and ever from one system to another, and that the duration of each will depend on the virtue of the subjects at the time.

The little worry locker, the holy of holies of the innermost economy of the soul, which is opened only at night. Everyone has his own.

In the dark ages, very great men often appeared. In those days only a man whom nature had expressly marked for greatness could become great. Now that education is so easy, men are drilled for greatness, just as dogs are trained to retrieve. In this way we've discovered a new sort of genius, those great at being drilled. These are the people who are mainly spoiling the market.

Probably no invention came more easily to man than inventing Heaven.

Her physical charms were precisely at that exact point where they begin to exchange their power of attraction for that of repulsion.

A punch in the stomach doesn't deprive the stomach of all consciousness, but the head itself. In general, people always talk of head and heart and much too little of the stomach, presumably because it's located

in the basement; but the ancients knew better. Persius*
awarded the stomach an M.A. – and since then it may
indeed have increased its learning.

When he philosophizes, he usually casts agreeable
moonlight over the objects treated. Generally it's
pleasing, but it doesn't show one single object distinctly.

On K's advice, I got frightfully angry about that
matter.

Even the gentlest, most modest and best girls are
always gentler, more modest and better when they've
found in the mirror that they've grown prettier.

What splendid shape the world would be in if the
great lords loved peace like a mistress! They have too
little personal reason to fear war.

Now reason 'stands out' above the realm of the
obscure but warm emotions like the Alpine peaks
above the clouds. They see the sun more clearly and
more distinctly, but they are cold and sterile. Reason
brags about its elevation.

Where everyone tries to come as early as possible,
the great majority must needs come too late.

I've again taken to eating all the forbidden dishes
and, thank God, feel just as bad as before.

* Roman satirist (A.D. 34–62).

How much depends on the way things are presented in this world can be seen from the very fact that coffee drunk out of wine glasses is really miserable stuff, as is meat cut at the table with a pair of scissors. Worst of all, as I once actually saw, is butter spread on a piece of bread with an old though very clean razor.

He kept continually polishing himself and finally became dull before he got sharp.

Now, in his old age, some mischievous ideas which he had printed seemed to him like the little spots which a beloved robin, while flying around his house, had made on his books, papers and furniture. Now that the little creature had been taken by a cat, it was forgiven for the spots.

Is reason, or rather the intellect, really better off when it arrives at final causes than when it arrives at a command of the heart? After all, it is surely a very open question which of the two ties us more strongly to the world surrounding us, the heart or reason.

Is it really so absolutely certain that our reason can know nothing metaphysical? Might man not be able to weave his ideas of God with just as much purpose as the spider weaves his net to catch flies? Or, in other words : might not beings exist who admire us as much for our ideas of God and immortality as we admire the spider and the silkworm?

I think one should think less about a science of

policing than a policing of science. Astronomy goes too far.

To reduce everything in man to simple principles means in the end, it seems, that we assume there *must* be such a principium – and how can this be proved?

LETTERS

Life In London
TO CHRISTIAN GOTTLOB HEYNE*

London, the 17th of April, 1770

Noble Sir,
Most Honourable Herr Hofrat,†

A week ago today, after a very fatiguing journey of fifteen days, I finally arrived in this enormous city, in better health than I had expected. It is incredible what an effect the crowd of new objects, which I have not always been able to fit into my head at once, has had on me. The most recent experience always made me completely forget the previous one, and I am still living, really, in such confusion that I, who formerly could fill sheets of paper with town gossip, am much perplexed about sifting out of my London experiences and the chaotic mass of things I could say enough material to fill a little letter. I have seen the sea, some warships of 74 guns, the King of England in the Houses of Parliament, in all his glory with the crown on his head, Westminster Abbey with the famous graves, St Paul's, the Lord Mayor moving with great state through a throng of many thousands, all shouting '*huzza, God bless him, Wilkes and liberty*' –

* Professor of Eloquence at the University of Göttingen; a famous classicist (1729–1812).

† Title of honour given to high government officials and eminent university professors.

and all this in a week. You, Sir, will easily believe that all this, happening at once, must be to such a retiring soul as mine what a week of university banquets and wedding parties, with no rest nor sleep, would be to my body. Moreover, I live in a house here where I have neither time nor repose to collect my thoughts, and as at a court I must dress twice a day, dine at 4.30 and often at 11.30 at night, usually in a large company

If one goes out, the distraction on the street is still greater; the tremendous uproar everywhere, the mass of new things wherever one looks, and the throng of chaises and people are the reason that one usually reaches one's destination late or not at all. Recently this happened to me : I went out with the firm resolution to go to see Herr Dieterich's correspondent in the Strand, but before I could get there I got stuck at silver shops, shops with wares from India, with instruments and the like, so that I barely had time to get home in time to dress, and Mr Elmsley's house was not reached on this expedition. The places I have looked at, I visited in Lord Boston's* chaise and in his company; otherwise I would perhaps still be lodged in an inn between here and St Paul's. Since I shall probably return to Göttingen with the young Adamses, and earlier than I thought, I'll save up all descriptions of what I've seen until then.

I would much like to stay here, but it would have to be under different circumstances. I have been received here in such a manner and treated with such respect as I could in no way expect; but this means that I had to accustom myself to a style of living

* His host. Lichtenberg had tutored one of Lord Boston's sons at Göttingen and was visiting England at his invitation.

which can never be mine in the future, for which it is too late anyway in my case, and which I utterly dislike. If I should actually begin to take pleasure in it, I would be completely lost. But it would be the more pleasant for me if I could live more to myself and more humbly, even if I were to pay for this happiness by performing tasks which I would not take upon myself at home. I already have some very eminent friends here, among whom I can also number Lord Marchmont, who recently spoke with me in public in the Houses of Parliament and next day, quite alone, visited me in my room, but I don't dare to make any such suggestion since I would certainly offend honest old Lord Boston gravely by so doing ...

I remain your very humble servant and friend,

G. C. LICHTENBERG

English Ladies
TO JOHANN CHRISTIAN DIETERICH*

London, the 19th of April, 1770

Dearest Friend,

I am infinitely obliged to you for being surety for me; you are a friend in need, of whom I have had very few. I hope soon to be back again, for I don't find things as advantageous as I'd thought, despite the fact that I'm really living what a Darmstadt head forester would call a blissful life : I wish that every honest fat man who travels to eat and drink were in my place. In

* Book dealer in Göttingen; Lichtenberg's publisher, landlord and lifelong friend (1722–1800).

a word, I live (against my will; that's the worst of it) really like a Prince Elector, and I'm convinced that if I lived this way a whole summer, my taste might perhaps be tuned too high and become eternally dissonant with my purse.

British food is simple, they say; that's true, you find few complicated dishes, but they have such a host of simple things that it would be foolish to combine them. In wines they are inexhaustible. First, they eat at midday, and then they drink at midday, two completely different things. At the latter occasion the women are no longer present – this for all sorts of reasons : firstly, so that they don't pilfer the secrets of state from the men; secondly, that no secrets are pilfered from them. At tea they come together again; it doesn't last long and each party keeps its secrets as best it can during this short time. In the evening, or in plain German at night, it's no better – I mean about eating and drinking; about the secrets it is definitely worse.

In London everything is for sale which you can't get for any money in other countries, and some you get quite free – all jumbled together at all hours of the day in all the streets, prepared in every manner, clothed, bound, framed, wrapped, unbound, rouged, preserved, raw, perfumed, in silk and in wool, with or without sugar. In a word, what man can't get here for money, he shouldn't look for in this real world.

Ordinarily I don't like to write about women, and I almost never do, unless the woman I write about, or the man I write to, is something extraordinary. Now I'm in a situation where both conditions hold, and so for once I'll really write myself out about women. As soon as one sets foot in England (I assume, however, that one has something besides feet), the extraordinary beauty of the women at once strikes the eyes of the student as well as the philosopher and the book dealer; and the number of these beauties increases continually, the closer one gets to London. For the man who is not really sure of himself in this respect, I know only one way out: let him at once go back with the next packet-boat to Holland. There he will be safe. In my life I have known very many beautiful women, but since I've been in England I have seen more than in all the rest of my life together, and yet I've been in England only ten days. Their extraordinarily pretty dress, which could give some appeal to a Göttingen fruit-woman, raises them still higher.

The housemaid who makes a fire in my fireplace every day and warms my bed (with a warming-pan, of course, friend) comes into the room at times with a black silk hat, at times with a white one and with a sort of train, carries her warming-pan with as much grace as some German ladies their parasols, and kneels before the bed in this costume with such nonchalance that you would think she had forty such trains; and at that, speaks an English which is hardly to be found in your best English books, my friend. If your heart can stand quite a bit, come over; I'll guarantee you'll be chattering English before your bed has been warmed forty times. All the streets teem with such creatures. The prettiest are the milliners (it was one of them who cost Lord Baltimore 120,000 thalers) and another species, of whom I have nothing to say except that there are no examples of their ever costing a man 120,000 thalers.

In a single hall, in the House of Lords, I've seen

over two hundred of the ladies of quality; imagine, two hundred, each of whom would have been worth at least 150,000 thalers to Lord Baltimore. This makes 200 times 150 thousand; that alone would be 30 million thalers, just the women as God made them without including a bit of diamonds and lace and pearls and such in the estimate. That is quite a capital sum! Now I really am tired of writing about the English women, and generally I think that if one can't stay here long, like me, it is better to look than to write. Meanwhile, I beg you not to include this report about English women in the *Gotha Calendar*,* not for my sake but for that of the German women. They don't mind if one praises the ladies of Lima as long as one wants to, but the English women are somewhat too close for them. History tells us that the men of Lower Saxony once before marched towards England *en masse*. Very profound political reasons are adduced as the cause, but we don't need them at all: the good Saxons were running away from their wives. So no word of my description must appear in the *Calendar* ...

Your most devoted friend and servant,

G. C. LICHTENBERG

Lonely in Hanover

Hanover, March 21st, 1772
Saturday morning at 8 o'clock

Dear Dieterich,

Good morning, for the first time from my new

* Published by Dieterich.

room, which is twice as large and twice as handsome as my other one.

God, what a peasant girl I just saw! She was wearing a fine napkin on her head, tied under her chin. I still can't understand how I know that she had a napkin around her head, for to the best of my knowledge I kept looking straight into her eyes and at her lips. Unfortunately she had nothing to sell which I needed, and vice versa: what I needed was not for sale. Good God, I thought, what are all the eye-salves of mortal apothecaries compared with Thine! – and with this thought I turned my eyes away, so that as little as possible of the salve should fall on my heart. I was on the point of answering your letter, and then the peasant girl came between us; now, since she's gone, let's get down to our work.

Here I don't even have a dog to whom I can say 'Du' (I have to put this down so abruptly to relieve my heart somewhat, which just swelled up at a certain thought). I wanted to buy myself a parrot today, but the fellow demanded six louis d'or; the creature would gladly have stayed with me. I will very willingly spend one louis d'or a month and hire someone whom I can call 'Du', who can be pinched in the cheeks and is made of fine stuff. If I don't soon do something about it, I already sense what things will be like: I'll read in the Bible four times a day, get yellow circles under my eyes and begin my letters with: 'Your Honoured favour has been received, if Your Esteemed self is still in good health,' etc.

My greetings to all our good friends, and be sure that I'll always be your faithful brother,

G. C. L.

A Provincial Party
TO MRS DIETERICH

Hanover, the 20th of May, 1772

Dearest Friend,

In order to tell you fully and properly how much your most charming letter pleased me, I'll briefly tell you the story of the day on which I received it. Note well how everything gets increasingly agreeable, and how fate has built over a foundation of annoyance a most elegant structure of agreeableness.

Seven in the morning, at the summer house.

SCHNEIDER.* Forgive me, are you already awake, Herr Professor?

THE PROFESSOR. Yes. 'Are you already awake?' I've already been awake for three hours. My head aches so atrociously. Did you bring the coffee?

SCHNEIDER. No! But the President of the Court sends you his regards and asks for the honour of your coming this afternoon for a cup of soup.

THE PROFESSOR. Oh hang it! That's what I thought. Everything has to happen at once (*turning his face to the wall again*), but I have no clean stockings.

SCHNEIDER. Yes, you have, sir.

THE PROFESSOR. Well, you know what to say, and bring the coffee – quick!

SCHNEIDER. Oh, I know what to say – and with that the cheerful fellow disappeared behind the scenes with his usual willingness, which was made doubly swift by the thought that he would have my four dishes to

* Lichtenberg's servant.

eat alone this afternoon. So much for the servant! But the master, he lay in bed, sleepy but unable to sleep, tormented by headache and still more by the sentence which had been pronounced on him : to have to dine *en gala* this afternoon with a large company.

Half past eight. Magistrate von Münchhausen enters the room. His intention was to tell me that he would pick me up at noon in his chaise, for he too was to dine at the President's. He stayed until around eleven, and during his visit I somewhat forgot that 'sentence'.

Quarter past eleven. I go into town; the sky clears up; my head does too, somewhat.

Half past eleven. The wig-maker falls upon me with his comb, and I with my knife upon a piece of bread and Limburger cheese, for dinner is not till two o'clock. He combs and I chew till a quarter past twelve. The day gets very fine, and I almost forget that I am to be taken to the place of judgment in three-quarters of an hour. Today is mail day, I thought, perhaps I'll get an answer. This thought makes it possible for me to rub my hands courageously and get dressed with all the self-denial of a philosopher.

One o'clock. I hear a chaise rattling up, and my heart changes its rhythm and shifts from an andante into a murky.* But it wasn't the right one, and I thank Heaven for this delay.

Ten minutes after one. O Lord, now another one rattles along as if the Devil himself were sitting on the coach-box, and it stops. Today is mail day, I said to myself. Professor, Heaven surely numbers all the beats

* A piece of harpsichord music, having a bass consisting of broken octaves.

of an anxious heart just as exactly as the hairs of our
head, and if It watches over sparrows, how much
more will It watch over a professor who, after all –
with the exception of one particular talent, perhaps –
is so much better than a whole spit full of sparrows. I
thought some such thing, and climbed into the
carriage.

Two o'clock. A large but very pleasant company at
the Herr President's. Five ladies were there; the professor sat between two of them. They must have been
of very noble birth for they didn't have a spark of
haughtiness, just as everything at the whole table
went on very amicably and agreeably, whereas behind our chairs stood eight to nine Presidents of the
Chamber, Privy Councillors and Field Marshals *en
livrée*. The one lady on my right was very young. She
probably made the great discovery of her vocation in
May or June (those are the right months for it), 1770;
thus she was probably sixteen. She had so transparent
a skin that I almost could have felt her pulse with my
eyes, I believe. Once, just as I was offering her a plate
of crab-tails, I brushed against her arm, down where
it joins the hand, with the outside of my right hand –
I can still show you the place. I wouldn't have
minded that it felt delicate, but it seems to me it was
so utterly fragile. The other, on my left, spoke a great
deal with me, was somewhat older, but encased in an
equally delicate skin. They seemed to be sisters, for
they called each other 'Du' at times, over my head,
and probably they hadn't drunk a pledge together.

Four o'clock. Two glasses of English beer, three
glasses of Rhine wine. It's getting finer and finer. The
sun is sinking, and I keep rising. Some cups of coffee,

standing up, and some very jolly talks with the honest old President.

Five o'clock. Leave-taking. (Not as hard as the one from Göttingen.) I get into the carriage with Herr von Münchhausen, and we drive down the lovely avenue to Herrenhausen. Here we get out and take a much-needed walk. Better and better! In every hedge a nightingale sat, so the poet says.

Seven o'clock. We fly to town, for the fellow drove like a young Englishman. I am set down at Herr Privy Secretary Schernhagen's, to whom I had been invited the day before. Now (finer and finer) he gives me your letter. I ran through it only hastily to see if it had any unpleasant news. That shall be my dessert, I thought, and sat down at a cheerful table. At eleven thirty I go to my quarters in town, read your letter a good ten times and go to my repose, which hadn't been over for a quarter of an hour when I took up my pen to tell you all this. This was the 19th of May, the day, I remember, when people in Darmstadt take the orange trees out of the greenhouses, and when the good season begins. Could I have celebrated it in a better way? ...

I remain with the most devoted friendship and the most consummate esteem,

Your utterly devoted servant,

G. C. LICHTENBERG

Pumpernickel and Girls
TO JOHANN CHRISTIAN DIETERICH

[*Osnabrück,* * *September or October,* 1772]

Dear Dieterich,

... It's now quite the wrong season to buy a ham; people generally have only one or two left which they won't gladly part with, or for only a high price.†

Pumpernickel, on the other hand, is always to be had, for the Westphalians pray daily: *give us this day our daily pumpernickel.* So you'll certainly get that, along with a pair of Westphalian dancing shoes which I've already bought – you shall do a dance in them for me when I arrive. If I come myself, I may also bring some ham. For you will barely be able to eat pumpernickel, and Christelchen‡ won't be able to at all; it's almost as if one were eating the grain raw. I have often tried and once had a piece served me which contained about twenty peasant-size bites. I bit some off with a serious air. 'Is it possible that you can't eat the bread as God made it, the bread that gives the peasant girls here their fine skin, liveliness and firm flesh?' I asked myself, and began to grind it between my teeth, for it never is milled. I chewed on; it was horrible. At times all the chewing made me laugh, and I gave the remaining 19½ bites to the horses. At times I indulged in devout contemplations: what a God that must be, who makes girl's flesh out of this sawdust. At

* In Westphalia, famous for its ham and pumpernickel.
† I swear that this is seriously meant.
‡ Dieterich's wife.

times my fancy became more daring: let's wait until the sawdust has been transubstantiated, then it will suit you better – but in any case the horses could count on the 19½ peasant-size bites. I haven't been able to make any more progress so far. The pumpernickel before its transubstantiation into —— is something ghastly, but after transubstantiation, something the like of which no mortal baker has ever baked or will bake. – So much about the pumpernickel and its trans-substantiation ...

Little Sybil
TO JOHANN CHRISTIAN DIETERICH

Oxenbridge, November 25th, 1772

O Friend,

If you could see how I sit here and write: my two feet put under my little Sybil, next to me another chair on which I'm writing; because of lack of space on the chair the inkwell is also under little Sybil, in my left hand I hold (it just came within a hair's breadth of falling!) a red-hot baked apple and suck at it. My right hand oscillates from the letter to the inkwell and from the inkwell to the letter, and the head (by which I mean me) doesn't worry a country library about what the hand is doing there. In any event I'm sitting warm. If only hard coal like this could be had in Göttingen too. A hard-coal stove is a real companion; and be-cause the little oven keeps me warm, costs money and I always find something in it to stir and stoke, I have devoted a sort of friendship to the thing and given it

83

the name little Sybil. Now let's see, what *was* it I wanted to say and – now I've forgotten it.

Assure Christelchen that she is in my good graces.

LICHTENBERG

'Oxenbridge' – I must remind you of this to save my honour – is not a pun fabricated by me, but this is actually supposed to be the origin of the name of Osnabrück.

A Sea Voyage
TO JOHANN ANDREAS SCHERNHAGEN*

Stade, the 19th of July, 1773

Day before yesterday at three o'clock I arrived at Brunswick happy but very tired, half roasted by the sun, with my mouth covered by blisters, clothing daubed with pitch, and a smell like a dried flounder, after a journey of eight days on sweet and salt water. I'd be able to fill a little book if I were to tell and describe for you, honoured Sir, all the pleasure, the heartfelt sadness, the views and curious little incidents which occurred on this trip – especially if I should pad a bit some of the least sentimental part with occasional remarks, as they would well deserve. So today I'll select only a few episodes here and there, with the solemn promise to supply all the rest in the future, if not in writing, then certainly by word of mouth.

The company, which had been decreased even on the day of departure by the prophecies and divinations of timid persons, consisted, at the end, of Captain

* One of the friends Lichtenberg made in Hanover in 1772.

von Hinüber, who had assumed the direction of the whole affair and to whom alone we were indebted for the great comfort, order and cleanliness on our ship; Lieutenant Zandré di Caraffa, a very courteous and withal most merry fellow, who played a great role during this trip; Lieutenant von Rönne, who had the strongest physique of us all and got seasick first; various other gentlemen; and – Me. Besides us there were the skipper with two sailors, three servants and a female cook – thus sixteen persons in all. We were equipped with provisions of all sorts; among other things, with a big cage full of chickens, and with guns, muskets, fire-crackers, shells and seven small cannon. For ballast we had taken on twenty large barrels filled with water, and two more with drinking-water. The cabin was divided into three parts by two rows of barrels; we dined in the centre, on the right were our bunks, and on the left the servants'. In fine weather we took coffee and tea on deck, facing in all directions, in all attitudes and positions.

From the start the wind was against us, so that we had to tack out to sea. Here it was against us too, but where it had seemed only to tease us before, it now proceeded to real violence; it blew so strongly, straight from Helgoland, that our pilot, whom we'd wisely taken on board earlier in Cuxhaven, said to our skipper: 'Listen, Skipper, we aren't getting anywhere, and I'm afraid tonight we'll get a stiff breeze.' We were actually at a place where a great many ships come to grief, so we turned right around and sailed before the wind to the Neues Werk,* where we dropped anchor and spent two nights and a day. Stay-

* A little island in the mouth of the River Elbe.

85

ing in this roadstead is particularly interesting, for at low tide we strolled as far as two miles from our ship, shot larks, snipe, caught crabs with our hands, mussels for the kitchen and for collections; and at high tide we sailed about in our longboat. At the end of the second night, a pleasant south wind set in with the ebb tide; in a short time it regained the ground we had lost before. At sea a calm beset us, but the weather was so pleasant that we, who had no interest in making money out of this journey, unanimously consider this day the most agreeable of our whole trip. The sea was all pearl-coloured, smooth as a mirror, and towards the west, beneath the sun, it seemed to be burning. The dolphins and seal accompanied our ship and for this honour were occasionally saluted with a bullet. We got to see all sorts of unusually shaped animals, and everywhere were the little shrimps, swarming like midges in the air and sunning themselves.

It may have been about six in the evening when Helgoland came in sight, and before it vanished in the dusk, it appeared dark blue against the red sky. As soon as it got dark, our south wind visited us again, and we were carried along swiftly to the island, off whose shore we cast anchor between 11 and 12 at night. About two miles before the island a barrel buoy is stationed to warn passers-by of a rock adjacent to it. You will believe without my mentioning it, Sir, that we all turned our attention towards discovering it in the dark, especially since our pilot had told us that same day that quite recently a ship had perished there. Passengers and sailors leaned down over the bow of the ship and looked for it. I *stood* behind them and looked over their heads and had the luck to see it first and called aloud: 'There's the buoy!' The helmsman, who saw it himself the next moment, altered his course slightly and we swept past; it was a joy to watch.

What made this night particularly remarkable to me was the phosphorescence of the sea water, which I had never seen before. It was not a matter of single sparks, say, or quickly vanishing faint flashes, but the foam on the waves seemed to glow in its entirety, which, since these waves were numberless, presented a display of fireworks probably as good as the one the artillery will set off at Hanover. To me at least, it was more attractive, much as I love fireworks, and I know your taste so well, Sir, that I am probably safe in maintaining that you would gladly have done without all the splendours of the artillery in return for my fireworks. I had a pail of it hauled up, and when I moved my hand in it the little waves shone in various places, approximately as an obliquely falling light tends to be reflected therein.

The pitcher which follows was filled by me from the fiery source; I'm forwarding it right away since the water in the pitcher could lose some of its quality before autumn. It will hardly shine any more, as even the sea does not shine in every wind. I shall be eager to hear what you, Sir, will say about its taste. – Barely had day broken when I crept on deck to see the true shape of the island, of which I'd formed all sorts of images along the lines of the little I had seen the day before. But its true shape surpassed all my imaginings by a very great deal. The whole island consists of a red, very much hardened marl, traversed by white veins. According to people's testimony, it towers 30 to 40 fathoms above the surface of the sea. The top soil on the island is not much more than four feet thick. The number of people is very large for this small place. Everywhere it teems with children, many of whom we saw going quite naked; they swim with a skill I'd never seen before. For three pennies, which I gave a ten-year-old boy, he swam quite a distance out to sea and turned over in the water so that only his feet could be seen; suddenly he turned another somersault, like a dolphin, and came up head-first.

A special kind of weariness, which I feel in this weather, prevents me from going into further detail. You will excuse, Sir, the confused way in which I have here related matters which are perhaps of no consequence ...

On the Power of Love
TO FRIEDERIKE BALDINGER *

Wednesday, 8 in the morning
February 19th, 1777

I can't continue the way I had begun yesterday, nor do I want to. So I'll lay a smaller foundation for a smaller building, for you to – blow down. Yet, to judge from a mysterious premonition, this letter won't turn out very short either; it will certainly turn out unusual. I'm risking a lot if I ever meant much to you, for I'm risking the loss of everything. You shall read

* Wife of Lichtenberg's colleague, Professor Ernst Gottfried Baldinger.

not only my thoughts on *falling in love* and the power of *woman* here in one epitome, but I want also to give you a brief sketch of my method of philosophizing, not merely to persuade you more easily about the first point, but that you may also more easily forgive me. I shall say everything in the most straightforward terms which occur to me, and must therefore ask for two things. First, that you imagine that I'm writing neither to *man nor woman*, but to a *soul* capable of reason. Then, since this concept might not be as familiar to many a person as it is to you, send back this letter, as soon as you've read it, again under seal. Only now I realize that one of these requests concerns your mind, the second your heart. Therefore I must add yet a third: that granting these requests should not depend on the attention which heart and mind will be able to pay to this *confusion*, for it might be that they would be utterly disappointed.

The question, 'Is the power of love irresistible?' or, in other words, 'Can the charm of one person affect us so strongly that inevitably we must fall into a state of misery, from which only the exclusive possession of that person can extricate us?' I've heard this answered with a 'yes' countless times by young and old. Often they raise their eyes to Heaven and fold their hands over their hearts, signs of deepest conviction and of nature's unconditional surrender. I too could answer with a 'yes'; nothing would be easier or cheaper, and in the future I'll do so again, to be polite. Possibly I'll do so seriously, if future experiences enrich the privy council from which I'm now philosophizing; but I doubt it very much, because a few examples, which

will battle on my side once they are properly eluci-
dated, suffice to refute the whole thesis for ever. As
I say, I've heard and read the thesis upheld countless
times, in prose and verse. But how many among its
upholders have seriously examined it? At least I'm not
aware that anyone has done so, and perhaps no one
really has; for who is likely to examine a matter to
whose truth the cuckoo and the nightingale, the turtle
dove, and the gryphon, bear witness with one voice –
at least, if one may believe the sweet and the bitter
bards of all ages. At their philosophy, however, the
philosopher fortunately laughs just as much as the
sensible girl laughs at their love. I have, I believe,
adequately explored this question.

I maintain with utter conviction: love's irresistible
power to make us either supremely happy or
supremely unhappy through one object is the poetic
twaddle of young persons whose mind hasn't attained
full growth, who don't yet have a voice in the council
of mankind in determining what is true, and who are
mostly so constituted that they won't ever be able to
have one. Here I declare again, although it's obvious,
that I don't mean the procreative urge; that *can* become
irresistible, I believe, but surely nature did not im-
print it on us to make us supremely unhappy or
supremely happy. To believe the former makes God a
tyrant, the latter makes man an animal. And yet all
the confusion in this dispute stems from not sufficiently distinguishing this urge, which appears in very
different forms, from rapturously sentimental love.
People defend love and attack love, and one party
understands one thing and the other something else.
That's all for this morning.

Thursday, 9 o'clock

Good-hearted maidens have taken the expressions *Heaven on earth* and *bliss*, with which many poets have labelled happy love, as eternal, unchangeable truth; and maidenish youths have believed it after them, though it's only the insipid chatter of young star-gazers who did not know what was heaven or what was earth. These appellations are true only to the extent that it's true that maidens are goddesses The Greeks, who were not only the wisest and bravest but also the most voluptuous people on earth, certainly did not think that girls were goddesses or that association with them was paradise or that their love was irresistible. They didn't even show them that respect for the weaker sex which one would have expected from a free people, not to speak of a tenderhearted one. They used them to breed those masses of organized flesh out of which they later formed heroes, sages and poets – and for the rest, let them go their own way. Women dwelt in the inmost part of the house and did not attend social gatherings with men. In this way, to be sure, they lost all opportunity to educate themselves up to the level of such clever persons, and so they had to become continually worse and more contemptible. That genuinely great men did pay court to some of them – this distinction they had first to earn through particularly outstanding intellectual talents, and these visits were not of the sort paid by men 'in love'. The Greeks did not reckon as a merit women's ability, bestowed by nature, to satisfy an urgent appetite in a pleasant and useful way. I think they were very much in the right, for it's a transaction in which both parties gain. The expressions *give away one's heart* or *one's favours*, again, are poetic flowers of speech. No girl gives her heart as a gift. She sells it either for money or for honour; or she exchanges it for another, an arrangement in which she has the better of it or at least thinks she has.

But why do I cite the Greeks to you? Does not a very sensible people exist today, free from the cult of enthusiastic love, which is both ridiculous and indolent; a people to whom alone we owe progress in useful studies, the improvement of man and all great deeds? Do you know which people I mean? Certainly, you're well acquainted with it. It is the community of active, reasonable, *vigorous* spirits which one finds spread over the whole earth, though many a town may have none of them: the healthy, useful, happy rustic whom our simple-minded poets celebrate and admire (as they do nature, as a matter of fact) without knowing him, and whose happiness they desire, without being willing to choose the way which leads to it. My blood boils when I hear our bards envying the happiness of the peasant. You want to be happy as he is, I'd always like to say, and at the same time stay the fop you are; that won't do at all. Work the way he does; if your limbs are too delicate for the plough, work in the depth of science; read Euler* or Haller† instead of Goethe, and bracing Plutarch instead of *Siegwart*.‡ Finally, learn to enjoy your rustic

* Leonhard Euler, famous Swiss mathematician (1707–83).

† Albrecht von Haller, Swiss scientist and poet, important in the history of physiology, botany, anatomy (1708–77).

‡ A sentimental novel by J. M. Miller, published in 1776, written in emulation of *The Sorrows of Young Werther*, the work by Goethe most widely known at that time.

girl like your rustic fare – transfigured and seasoned by hunger – as your peasant does. Then you'll be happy, as he is.

Not nobility of soul nor sensitivity, but idleness (or at least work which leaves the mind idle) and ignorance of the great attractions of science, in which there is absolutely nothing about *love and wine*, are the sources of that dangerous passion, which never – I'll venture this as a general statement – has gained power over a truly manly soul. If love makes a person seek out the wilderness and chat with the moon in all seriousness, he certainly has a screw a little loose somewhere, for one weakness seldom occurs alone.

I have very lofty ideas of the greatness and dignity of man. To follow an urge without which the world could not endure; to love the person who has chosen me as her only companion, especially since, according to our customs, this person clings firmly to my heart by a thousand other things, and influences me in the varied relationships of adviser, friend, business associate, bed-comrade, plaything, jolly brother (sister doesn't sound right) – that surely I consider no weakness but clearly plain duty; also, I don't think it's within our power not to love such a creature. But that a girl should be able by her charms to steal a man's peace, so that he would have no taste for any other pleasure, and that it should not lie within his power to resist this inclination – not in the power of a man who can bear poverty, hunger, scorn of his own merit, go to his death for honour's sake? – that I'll never believe. It may be true for the fop, the soft weakling who has never tried to resist in any matter, or the voluptuary who knows no higher pleasure of the mind than the consciousness that a pretty girl loves him, but certainly not for a man of real soul. If such a man ever made a statement of that sort, it was a compliment to the ladies, indeed a very impolite one, because it's a lampoon against all reasonable men; and yet it's a question if it is a compliment to the ladies at all. Many men think the female sex so weak, vain, credulous and conceited that they believe everything they're told if it concerns the power of their charms. But these men, if one can call them that, are very greatly in error. Don't you agree, Madam?

But if we capriciously indulge in a notion based on such an urge, and not only don't try to resist it but are even proud of not resisting, and think ourselves initiates into the mysteries of all-delighting nature as soon as we can build such love-castles in the air – Oh God, what wouldn't be called irresistible in this world!

The love which I think proper for a reasonable man is related to the kind against which I write, as the just tear shed by the true man at his mother's death is to the ill-bred howling and tearing of hair of the weak-souled mob. And I know well, even if I preached till Judgment Day, the number of those who steadfastly resist those consequences of love will always be the smaller. But why should that be more surprising than that the people who bear their misfortunes with courage and calm are likewise very few? We must not base our conclusions of what man might be someday on what he is in Europe today. On other continents he is indeed different, far different ...

The Death of Dorothea Stechard*
TO A. L. F. MEISTER†

[*Göttingen, the middle of August,* 1782]

My dear Colleague,

What do you say about our household? Two hours after my excellent girl had been carried away, the little Dieterich girl died. Every hour they asked about each other's health, and their graves are close to each other. The little Stechard girl became a victim of the SCIENCE OF MEDICINE. We can consider that a fact. I put up with everything, for I foresaw that if she died anyway, what a terrible torture it would be to have to face the reproach that she would still be alive if the doctors' directions had not been followed. This struggle was the hardest for me.

Everything is over, and I am trying hard not to think of the past any more, and gradually I am beginning to acquire some skill in this. So I beg you, Sir, to do me the honour and kindness of visiting me, and, in fact, if it won't inconvenience you, next *Saturday and next Sunday* for supper. You'll find me on a different storey, in one of the rooms I used to live in, and Herr Dieterich is with me. We sleep in the same room. Please don't refuse my request. You shall not be troubled by my weeping or complaining – I'm now

* See following letter. Lichtenberg had met her in 1777, selling flowers, when she was eleven or twelve years old. He gave her work as a kind of maid and taught her the elementary school subjects. In 1780 she moved into his apartment. From then on, they lived as man and wife.

† Albrecht Ludwig Friederich Meister, Professor of Mathematics at the University of Göttingen; formerly Lichtenberg's teacher, then his closest friend among his colleagues.

beyond all that – and whining to my friends has never been my way. So I'll definitely expect you the day after tomorrow at seven in the evening; I think that all your friends with whom you might have previous engagements would gladly yield to me under the circumstances. The little Dieterich girl would have been twenty-one years old next August 31st. If I had only kept my girl that long. She died four years younger.

G. C. L.

TO FRANZ FERDINAND WOLFF*

Göttingen, the 19th of August, 1782

Heaven has brought my anxieties to an end, but in a way which has subjected me to great torture, deeply convinced though I am of the infinite wisdom with which it has chosen this way rather than others. The two have died: Mademoiselle Dieterich in her twenty-first year; and she who was my closest concern, a girl of unusual intelligence and heavenly goodness of disposition, whom I had educated completely according to my own ideas, after living seventeen years and thirty-nine days. My sleepless nights and my grief brought on an illness which has kept me prostrate since last Tuesday; I have neither been allowed nor able to get up. Now the machine is moving again; for how long, only He who was pleased to ruin its movement knows … Very soon you will hear more from

Your most devoted servant,

G. C. LICHTENBERG

* Met Lichtenberg in Hanover in 1772 and became his friend; they shared their interests in physics and chemistry (1747–1804).

A Thunderstorm
TO FRANZ FERDINAND WOLFF

Göttingen, July 21st, 1783
4 o'clock in the afternoon

My dear friend,

At just this moment the first snatch of sunshine is appearing again after a frighteningly beautiful thunderstorm with hail; the tiles are still dripping. This time I felt no small anxiety for our town. As the storm approached, it got almost dark and every flash of lightning was a blow. Actually I am not a sentimental sort, at least not in public: I enjoy in silence and let others chatter about it. But truly I am still so full of this great spectacle that the other things I wanted to tell you, which would have been *all* I'd have told you this morning, can't get expressed at all until I've told you something about my feelings. The day was oppressively hot and I was extremely sensitive; moreover, this is the anniversary of my father's death, on which I ordinarily shut myself away. Nothing in the world could correspond better with my feelings than such weather. When the thunder once rolled so deep that I thought it was *under* me, I never, I may say, felt my own nothingness more keenly than in that moment. Truly, tears came to my eyes – tears merely of admiration and heart-felt devotion. There can be nothing greater and more majestic. I don't know – I now feel unusually light; it is as if I had paid off a great debt and as if the spirit of my father were rejoicing that I observed so unhypocritical an hour of

G

prayer on his anniversary. Now it has been said, and now I am back to my usual pace.

Fortunately the storm moved rapidly. The next peal of thunder followed the lightning in three seconds, so it might well have struck here, but I heard nothing about it. There was only a little hail; no window-pane within my range of vision was broken, but it made quite a clatter on the tiles. The street, though, looked like the Leine.* The pigs look as clean as humans, and the humans, like pigs.

The storm is leaving, and the girls are appearing at the windows vertically.

I have the honour of remaining *in nebula nebulorum*.

G. C. L.

Volta
TO FRANZ FERDINAND WOLFF

Göttingen, the 22nd of November, 1784

Dearest Friend,

... I do indeed regret that you did not speak to Volta. He is an extraordinary man. DeLuc is right: he wrote me once *qu'en Electricité Volta voyoit avec les yeux de Newton*. He is full of ideas and a *raisonneur* without peer. He had many instruments along; he unpacked them for me, and during his stay here I kept them in my own quarters. They are locksmith's work, but he accomplished everything with them. He stayed here

* River on which Göttingen is situated.

five days, and two-thirds of them, certainly, he spent in my room. My experiments with aerial electricity pleased him incredibly. For I let an 18-inch balloon rise out of the window on a thread of silk woven together with silver and investigated the electricity of the air, on my table, in all ways. I struck suns two inches in diameter. Watching, he was overtaken by his own ideas, and he actually did not hear or see some aristocratic students whom I introduced to him formally. The next day he came at dawn and made preparations to repeat the experiments himself, which he actually did. On that morning the air was so still that the balloon on my balcony hung three hundred feet high, directly above our heads. I had stretched a silk ribbon across the balcony doorway; the balloon string was wound around this and thus led over to the table. So away with kites in the future, at least for class purposes. I can't stand the field trips with the 'fellow-students'.

Then he wanted to show me an experiment to prove that fumes carry away positive electricity. He insulated a brazier containing a few dimly glowing coals, wet a linen rag and threw it on the coals; he had run a wire from the brazier to a very sensitive electrometer. But nothing happened. He cursed in French and Italian; but since, as you know, curses are little if any help on such occasions, there was no improvement. That afternoon I repeated the experiments with the *Aeolipia* and then with ether, and they went splendidly. At least I got a *Voyés Vous* for thanks. He is a handsome fellow, and during some extremely uninhibited hours, at a supper at my place when we talked wildly till about one o'clock, I noticed that he has an expert knowledge of the electricity in girls ...

I have the honour to remain, with sincere esteem, Sir,

Your most obedient servant,

G. C. LICHTENBERG

A Thwarted Plan
TO JOHANN GOTTWERT MÜLLER *

Göttingen, December 20th, 1784

Your short but excellent letter gave me a very great deal of pleasure. As for your friendly sharing in my joy at the journey to Italy, however, I've made a small, permissible change. I have kept its total value but reversed its meaning. Alas, my journey has come to nothing – not only quite without fault of mine, but even with a little loss of five hundred thalers. I had money, indeed considerably more than was needed for carriage grease and for oats; I had permission, health and courage – but my friend and travelling companion, the Danish Finance-Counsellor Ljungberg, of Copenhagen, had not taken enough trouble about arranging for leave. He was kept up in the air, and finally, after I had long since given up all my lecture courses, paid back sixty gleaming louis d'or and waived my claim to forty others, he was refused. I thought I would fall to the floor. In fact, though I have never been out of my mind, I now know how a

---

* Book dealer in Itzehoe; wrote satirical novels which Lichtenberg greatly admired (1743–1828).

man feels when he is on the point of frenzy, and that is the only profit I've had in this matter.

I had prepared myself for the journey for more than nine weeks, crossed the Rubicon with Caesar, the Alps with Hannibal and with Constantine the bridge where the sacred cross stood in the sky. I climbed up the Capitol, touched the prows of the ships and felt giddy on the Tarpeian Rock. – In the second act appeared the Laocoön, the Apollo Belvedere and the Medicean Venus in Florence; all the walls were hung with Raphaels and Correggios. – In the third I clambered up Vesuvius, went for a walk among the Pontine swamps, which have recently been burned over, saw the Styx and the Cave of the Dog, and walked down avenues of blooming aloe and orange trees – and suddenly, as if lightning had struck, nothing was there for my whole winter except Göttingen snow, the ringing of sleigh bells and the scrawny hyacinth bulbs by my window.

But, friend, the journey is only delayed; next September I'll quite certainly make it if I can find companionship, of which there's no doubt. It has long been my carefully considered axiom : no one who can go there must fail to see Italy. That journey is strength for body and soul.

You were anxious about me because of winter. No, my dear fellow, Italy must be seen in the winter. In the first place, one plays hooky for a whole winter – which is really no trifle for people like us – and goes for walks among the flowers, while certain people in Itzehoe, whom I won't name, admire the lovely icicles in their beards. And then, Italy is really too hot for us in the summer and very unhealthy unless one is willing and able to spend months in some of the *un-interesting* regions. Between Rome and Naples, the orange trees are already along the highways; there, I think, the song 'A Child is Born in Bethlehem, Bethlehem' can be struck up without fuss and foot stoves. If you could come along, dearest friend, what a joy that would be! One ought to have eight hundred thalers (apiece, I mean), and for that we would see Dresden, Prague, Vienna, Trieste, Venice, Milan, Turin, Pavia, Bologna, Florence, Rome, Naples, perhaps Calabria and Messina; on the way back *Loretto*, Lucca, Livorno, the Alps, Geneva, Lausanne, Berne, Zürich, Basle, etc. What a harvest for you, who are certainly on the way to becoming our Fielding* – and more! What psychological views you could collect. For a man like you, the book dealer must pay the travel costs ...

Congratulations to a New Father
TO GEORG HEINRICH HOLLENBERG†

Göttingen, November 13th, 1785

Noble Sir,
Right Honourable General County Surveyor
Praiseworthy, graduated Papa!

Bravo, bravo! dear friend. That's the way. Marriage today and in a year – crash, bang, baptism! What good, otherwise, are all learning and all canal build-

* Henry Fielding, English novelist, author of *Tom Jones* (1707–54).
† Ten years younger than Lichtenberg; was a civil engineer in Osnabrück when Lichtenberg stayed there in 1772.

ing? Papa Hollenberg – that sounds so splendid to me that I have probably said it ten times today, and once out of the window, so that all the world could have heard it. – Oh, do write me how you look now! Is it really true that when a man becomes a papa he must acquire a big peruke, wear a figured dressing-gown, and a belt, and yellow slippers and at times stand in the window with his long pipe in his mouth and his pipe tamper on his little finger; and whether another dressing-gown is needed for Sundays; also, whether he must cross the street more slowly than before, and how much time you now need, say, to go from the gate of the Kaiser Inn to the new city-hall stairs; and whether he may read the evening blessing in the same tone as before without coughing when he begins; and whether at night he has to sleep on the side of the bed where the cradle is standing, or whether he may lie down on the far side next to the wall; and whether it is absolutely necessary to be a model for the servants in the house, especially the maids, with earnest face and good example? You see, my dear fellow, these are cardinal questions which, if they are properly answered in my case, might yet bring me some day to the position where you now are.*

All joking aside, my dear Hollenberg, your letter really gave me a pleasure which moved me to tears. I see that you are happy; what you have told me of your admirable wife proves this beyond contradiction, and I take so much real interest in everything that

* Written tongue-in-cheek: the birth of Lichtenberg's first child by Margarete Kellner, his common-law wife, was less than three months away. Georg Christoph, Jr, was born on February 4th, 1786.

concerns you that your happiness always constitutes no small part of mine. Keep your fondness for me as it has been, and gain me the friendship of your wife, who must be high-minded, from the few lines I have seen. And if some day you are again delighted by a little girl who is heavier by half an ounce or so – that's what we wicked unmarried sinners call the little boys – then dedicate this *puellam cum appendice* to

Your

most faithful friend

G. C. LICHTENBERG

The Good Life
TO GOTTFRIED HIERONYMUS AMELUNG*

Göttingen, March 24th, 1786

My best friend!

I give you this name with all the fullness of my heart, for none of my friends, not excepting even my brothers, treat my inexcusable negligence in letter-writing with the heavenly forbearance with which you deal with it. You can't believe how great the very particular emotion was with which, therefore, I read your excellent essay in the *Church Herald* about a week ago. At every line I thought: Look, what an excellent man you have offended. I was also really on the point of asking you for your absolution in a circumstantial confession, when your kind letter came; it revived my spirits and gave me assurance that I

* One of Lichtenberg's schoolmates, who became a minister.

could again write directly to my Amelung without making this tiresome confession of my sins.

Yet I do owe you the following confession: I have a great deal to do, even though I lecture only three hours a day. The nature of my lectures does not require the usual preparation, like dogmatics, say, or Pandects, etc. Rather, the numerous instruments which have been unused for half a year often have to be looked for among the great many we own; they must be properly set up when they are found, and frequently even repaired, for there are some at which the tooth of time, and those of the mice and moths, very soon begin to gnaw – not even to mention the fingers and elbows of the ignorant servants. Thus the days pass. Moreover, my friends here who know my duties also know which hours I am free, for which I am very grateful to them, and visit me on Sundays or in the evenings. When I am alone I am frequently very tired, or find myself obliged to catch up with the latest achievements in my field, lest I fall behind. Seldom, anyway, am I in the proper mood without which one must never write to Amelung. You see, that's about how things are with me – forgive me.

What is my dear little friend up to? Is he already falling nicely? And breaking things nicely? The former is a very good sign, only one must try to arrange that it always takes place on his behind, which exists mainly for that purpose. While I don't grasp the psychological reason, it is certain that man is an animal which must, if it is to reach its destination, be attacked first at its behind, until its 10th year, and then at its head. I conceive of behind and head as the poles of the magnetic needle, which, however opposed to each other they may be, have yet a great affinity between them. – What can I send the dear little fellow? Just tell me. You know our exports: sausage and compendia. Would they be welcome? Say the word!

The ideas you expressed about religion and – THEOLOGY in your last letter to me pleased me vastly. They are so very much my own that I could almost believe that you had looked into my Ledger, in which I usually enter my little intellectual income penny by penny, every day. But of course a man of your intellect and active benevolence, the sort which can exist only where there's sincere conviction, does not need to look into the ledger of a professor – and a layman at that! – to learn such things. Meanwhile, quiet in the harbour, I calmly watch all the troubles of life and am convinced that after all they finally *help* to lead us towards the great goal of our true destiny. Since we cannot see very far beyond our own position, the best way can be found only through experiments. With this method, to be sure, many a man will perish in the morass which his successor will avoid just because he has perished there. In the long run everything will be clear and good, if only we love one another, and each one, with practised understanding, tries to do as much good as he can. If I were ever to publish a sermon, it would certainly be about the great ability that everyone, be he who he will, has to do good, without wasting anything. People of all stations, all over the world, fail to realize their importance in this respect. In this regard, everyone, whoever he is, is a prince in his own situation. The devil take our existence here on earth if only the Emperor could do good. That is the Law of the Prophets. Something of this, I think, ought to be included in every sermon. You are the man who shows this through his example: what an impression would it not make, if you taught this from the pulpit and demonstrated in DETAIL how everyone could play a similar part in his own situation!

Now an affair which occurred three nights before last in our house and is indeed completely unprecedented here and really terrible. It took place on my storey, but since I live in one of the largest houses of the town, it happened so far from me that I heard nothing at all of the thing while it was going on. In this storey a Count Breuner of Vienna, the son of the Imperial Ambassador to the Republic of Venice, has accommodations with his tutor, Captain Burdell; both are men of the highest character. They wanted to depart at Easter, and received last week their monies for the journey and for paying their bill, about 2,000 thalers in louis d'or at five. The rabble here found out about this; generally it acquires information very much faster than do the leaders of our police. So on the night mentioned, six or seven masked fellows broke into the Captain's room, tied him up in bed with ripped-up curtains, hunted the keys quite calmly and escaped with all the money, after threatening to set the house on fire if he made the slightest noise. Actually the rug did start to burn, which fire the Captain, who hurled himself out of the bed, rolled out with his own body. – Isn't this a hideous affair, especially in a house in which at least fifty to sixty people are asleep, and in a sleepy little place like Göttingen?

A Fire
TO JOHANN DANIEL RAMBERG*

Göttingen, August 6th, 1786

Noble Sir,

... Now one more small but sad affair, of which I am still much too full to keep quiet about. In the night from August 4th to 5th, I was awakened at 12.30 by the cry of *Fire!* When I opened my eyes, my bedroom was as bright as if the sun were shining, and before I could locate the sleeves of my dressing-gown, the colour rose to a pinkish red. It was directly opposite me. But I quickly got hold of myself, ran for my bit of money and only then looked into the matter further: I found the gable of a house wrapped in flames, and I felt the warmth. There was little wind, however, and what little there was, was favourable to me, so I ordered that none of my things were to be saved, and it turned out fortunately. A hose operated by an air-chamber worked so splendidly that I laughed and shed tears of joy; it was a strange sensation.

On this occasion I found an observation confirmed which I had already made before. The danger of fire, and perhaps and presumably every danger, is more terrible to the imagination than *in re*; we usually think of such things when body and soul are ill disposed. When the danger is actually at hand, brooding, the product of coddling and idleness, disappears, and one becomes a man of action who keeps his eye

* Army Counsellor in Hanover, Lichtenberg's friend from 1772 on.

only on *res facti*. I was cautious and alert, completely calm and ready for all eventualities.

I was uncommonly pleased that the princes'* tutors came to my room and stayed till the end. The next morning princes and tutors sent inquiries about how I was, and when the princes were passing by the following evening and I was leaning out of the window, they rushed up below it and called up to me about the incident. They themselves were wisely allowed to sleep through it, for though they dwell in the same building as I, their quarters face on another street ...

A Message to a Godchild
TO GEORG HEINRICH HOLLENBERG

Göttingen, the 23rd of September, 1788

Dearest Friend,

For Heaven's sake, don't interpret it as negligence that I am rather late in answering your valued letter. Actually I should have said: my dear, kind friend, explain to your beloved wife that the slight delay of my answer does not stem from negligence. For *you* know me, I know, and you know how much everything which concerns you interests me, and how much I am pleased by each incident which brings me into a closer relation with you and your family.

* King George III's three younger sons studied at the University of Göttingen. They had been introduced to Lichtenberg as children, in 1775, when he was a guest of the king's family. Now he lectured to them privately six times a week. Two of the princes roomed in Dieterich's large house, where Lichtenberg was also a tenant.

Long live the *Dauphin*, *Bernhard the First*, and his gallant parents, therefore, and a thousand thanks for the honour of being made godfather. I actually wanted to write to the little fellow himself, and I did not consider till very late that he would hardly be able to read the letter. It began thus: Welcome, dear little one, in this vale of tears! I am uncommonly pleased to see you here. But be careful: you can't possibly believe what a hole it is, this world. If you want to be happy, for Heaven's sake stay on the highway with your wagon; otherwise you will run the risk that the priests will unharness your horses, and there you will sit. *Or more briefly:* act in all respects like your worthy father and in as few as possible like your worthy godfather; then you can't go wrong. Moreover, don't cry too much. Be quiet especially at night, and bear in mind that your good mother wants to sleep too, and that during the day, when you're asleep, she has other things to do.

When you begin to walk, I, of course, allow you to fall down, for a regular boy falls at least three times a day. But just don't fall on your so-called pate, for *that* God gave you to write compendia; and not on your nose, for that serves to set spectacles on. Rather you will soon find that Nature equipped you in the middle of your body (N.B., towards the rear) with two cushions, which are called buttocks. Look, dear boy, these two things have no use in the world except the following, which can conveniently be arranged in four groups:

1. During the study of the Latin language and of Christianity, or when naughty, in the beginning to be

whacked with the hand, and in more mature years with the rod.

2. To fall on it. So when you notice that you would fall on your head, you make a leap and fall on your respective falling-mats.

3. To let yourself down on them or, as one says, to sit down. For since the chairs of the Patriarchs were of wood or stone, Nature had to attach the cushions to the body. Today, when people, the upper class particularly, frequently lose these natural pillows, buttocks have been attached to the chairs themselves.

4. And that is a principal use. If some nasty fellow is reviling you and does not even have the guts to stand up to you until you've been able to box his ears, open your coat in the rear and show him your cushions. In learned controversies, this type of self-defence is not valid; scholars have a very special backside, usually called *moral*, which does not lie at the centre of their system. How people show it to each other, you will learn at the universities, where there is abundant opportunity for mutual instruction; this science is called polemics.

Dearest friend, excuse me for this little joke; it was inspired only by the joy caused by your admirable letter, which is lying open before me; I could give you no better evidence of the sincerity of my feelings than the sort I furnished. For even 'Guides for Letter Writers' have the *words* for an answer, just as today buttocks of deer and horse hair and eiderdown are buckled on the chairs and armchairs; yet lack of feeling cannot be replaced by affectation ...

Now, dearest friend, give my most cordial regards

to your dear wife and to the *Dauphin*. I remain, in true friendship and devotion, always

Yours,

G. C. LICHTENBERG

To a Little Boy
TO GEORG HEINRICH HOLLENBERG

Göttingen, September 2nd, 1793

Dearest friend,

You must by all means forgive me if I do not honour every draft which your love draws on me in the currency which you demand. I mean, if I don't immediately answer your letters with letters. The hardest thing for my heart is to raise precisely this sort of conventional money. If you would visit me some day, man closest to my heart, I would tell you stories, read to you, wait on you hand and foot; I would kiss your dear children and, with the permission of the authorities, your charming wife too. I would do and say a thousand things, and have a thousand done and said, from which you could tell how much I love you and with what precision I answer your letters, in silent gratitude. But to write letters, *write* with pen and ink on paper, that, that, you wonderful fellow, is as hard for me at times as jumping over a fence. But of course if it goes on that way, one must –

Yet for this a new, clean sheet is needed,

so turn over.

Dear little Hermann Hollenberg, I send you a

thousand greetings because of your fine parents, whom I love and to whom you are bringing so much joy and, if you are obedient, will continue to do so. But allow a few words to me, an old friend of your worthy father and one who has some acquaintance with the world. I see that you have no trousers on; men of that sort are now called *sans culottes*; and by that, people in many sections of your German fatherland mean the Satan's spawn of liberal intellectuals, philosophers, teachers of the people and free-thinkers – in a word, all those who do not devote themselves to chasing golden snuff-boxes.* Now although it's no disgrace to come into the world without trousers, as you did – or, like your father's friend, soon to leave it without having any on – do cover your nakedness with this necessary garment as long as you wander about in this world. Have it so cut that if possible it will cover your eyes and ears, and wear your head inside your fly too, and then you will never want for anything. Above all things, though, my dearest child, endeavour – My God, what am I saying? I didn't stop to think that it is no longer wise to dispatch truths by mail, so the rest orally some day. Oh! joking aside, your domestic happiness has meant a thoroughly lovely charming evening for me. If only I had the patience and energy to write!

For hours I have been looking for your last letter to answer some points raised in it; with my impatient nature I've been unable to find it. Since just today I am somewhat in the mood to write, the letters are crowding upon me so terribly that I must close. Remember

* Presumably given by one's superiors as tokens of recognition.

me to the dear new mother, and your little *sans culottes* Arminius, and all the others most cordially, and do not forget me,

Your

faithful

G. C. LICHTENBERG

After an Illness
TO JOHANN GOTTWERT MÜLLER

Göttingen, July 16th, 1794

Honoured Sir and Friend,

I don't know whether you have heard that at the very time, even on almost the same day, that the revolution broke out in France a most remarkable one broke out in my body and my domestic life. I got married, and that is the fine side of the upheaval; I was attacked by a convulsive asthma which threatened me with suffocation almost daily for more than four weeks, that is the ugly side. On the first part I will say no more, dearest friend, than that I live most happily and pleasantly, and have four children running about me, who, thank God, are all very healthy. With my admirable wife they make my life so very delightful that I look back on the portion of it when I could have been married but was not as on a half-savage state. This goes so far that, just as Cato used to end his letters with *Carthaginem esse delendam*, I always end mine to unmarried friends with *uxorem esse ducendam.**

* 'A man must marry,' a parody of 'We must destroy Carthage'.

But of the second part, my dear friend, I have more to say. If it had been only a matter of the four aforesaid weeks, I would barely have mentioned it and by no means would have called it a revolution. After that attack I was bedridden, and was lying down literally a full half year of $365 \div 2$ days, lived mainly on medicines at that time, did recover, to be sure, but how? *Eheu quantum mutatus ab illo!** Truly our transfigured body, on the day of resurrection, cannot be as different from the buried bag of maggots in the earth as the reconvalescent *Hofrat* was from the one who had been put to bed $365 \div 2$ days before. Only with the vast difference that the transfigured one stayed in bed and the bag of maggots got up. My gaiety, my fearlessness, my carefreeness, my love of reading and of writing at least for myself, all that stayed in bed and now is gone.

All my present life seems to me so lacking in coherence in itself and with its earlier portion that you would hardly take it for the index of what preceded it, if you looked at it through my eyes. I began to consider myself as an entirely different person and literally believed that the bag of maggots was not obliged to pay the debts which the transfigured one had contracted. So my whole correspondence began to come to a halt. When I still wrote letters, they were always those in which something appeared, at least in the postscript, which served to feed the *fire* in the *kitchen*, or where I could have been prosecuted legally for dilatoriness. The pen from which many a joke for my friends used to flow, now produced almost nothing

---

* 'Alas, how much he has changed!' In the *Aeneid*, Aeneas says this of the dead Hector, who appears to him in a dream.

anymore but *valutas, usances* and *at sights*;* at least
I don't know how to express more briefly what it
wrote than by these words, the most unaesthetic I can
imagine. Here, best of men, you have the data for an
introduction to this renewed correspondence with you,
which† I do not wish to pursue further now. I shall
add only this one thing, that I find my condition
VERY, VERY much more tolerable in this fertile year
of storms and have hope that I shall be reborn.

You, good man, warm friend, and (German)
FIELDING‡ have never been absent from my heart,
either after my resurrection or before my decease. I
read your letter not without deep emotion. If Dieterich
had been here then (I could not write a complete
answer in his absence) I would have answered at once,
but he stayed away for a long time. When he came,
my dreadful indolence set in again with the south-
ing-hot (I meant to write 'seething hot', but let it
stand) weather, and so the answer was not written
until today. Now your excellent friend volunteers to
take it to you.

Dieterich is certainly your friend now as ever. A
certain negligence, which has always been characteristic of him, and a certain failing of his memory, in
which alone his old age shows, and all sorts of
domestic circumstances of the saddest sort have oc-
casioned several stoppages like the one between you
and him. Thank God, however, the prosperity of his
business has not decreased. He is ineffably devoted to

---

* Terms used in writing out bills of exchange and notes.
† *Videlicet* the introduction, not the correspondence.
Videatur contextus.
‡ Lichtenberg compares Müller to the English novelist.

you and believes that you had forgotten him. Please don't forget him, and bless his press again. I know that he will eagerly pick up even the crumbs which fall from your table, for it hurt him a great deal when you sent your delicacies to Berlin and Stettin.* If you wish to admit him to favour again, do let me handle the matter.

Truly, dearest friend, I am astonished at the inexhaustibility of your genius. In little Itzehoe, you carry a whole London in your head. Do tell me how you manage that and what sort of Herschelian† invention you have made, so that in the little town where you live you look so deeply and rightly into the world that its circumnavigators lag behind you. Perhaps I shall take occasion very soon to express publicly, even if only in a few hasty lines, thanks for the pleasure you have afforded me. To be sure, it will not be done merely out of gratitude but (this is only whispered) to tell the public that I know this man and that he is my friend.

What is my dear godson up to? Is he coming to Göttingen soon?

Well, my dearest friend, remember me to your estimable wife, of whose praise everyone who comes from there is full, and remain the friend of

Your

always faithful

G. C. LICHTENBERG

To Herr Fielding-Müller.

* Towns where some of Müller's books were published.
† In 1781, when still an unknown astronomer, Sir William Herschel (1738–1822) discovered the planet Uranus with a telescope of his own construction. This and his subsequent discoveries attracted world-wide attention.

Lichtenberg's Last Letter
TO LUDWIG CHRISTIAN LICHTENBERG*

Göttingen, the 18th of February, 1799

My dear brother,

... Your anti-Kantianism really delighted me, since I know now how you see the matter. As a person he is certainly a great man – and what is certainly just as important, a well-intentioned, worthy one. His *Critique of Pure Reason* is the work of 30 years of study. He has given lectures on systems of philosophy for a long time; this, to be sure, made him familiar with a great many things with which countless people, even men of real intellect, are not – at least not to the same degree. Therefore he often does not seem to be clear until one becomes familiar with his thought. Therefore even K——† often knows nothing to adduce against him except that Leibniz, say, said something similar 100 years ago. But Kant does not pass himself off as the discoverer of everything either; he only interrelates what great men said and thought singly long ago, and (N.B.) shows why we must think and speak in that way. It's well known that Aristarchus of Samos taught, more than 1000 years before Copernicus, that the sun stood still and the earth revolved about it, but those were only single rays of light which were lost in the surrounding waste of darkness. Kant once alludes to some such matter – in the preface to his

* One of Lichtenberg's elder brothers.

† A. G. Kästner (1719–1800), Professor of Mathematics at Göttingen and Lichtenberg's teacher, wrote satirical epigrams. He was disliked by Lichtenberg and many others for his vanity and his domineering manner.

Critique of Pure Reason, if I'm not mistaken – with great delicacy. The comparison stands up. Up to now we have believed that we were the product of things outside of us, of which we knew and could know, after all, nothing except what our Ego reported to us. What, then, if it were precisely the nature of our being that actually makes this world? Here the revolving and rotation of the earth around its axis are opposed to the revolving of the sun and the host of stars around it. Indeed, he puts everything to the test. A dogmatizing Kantian is surely not a genuine one. Even Fichte, *quod pace tua dixerim*,* has offended more against discretion than against philosophy. It was culpable mischievousness in him, it seems to me, to speak the way he did, and will probably always be. We more refined Christians look down upon the worship of images; i.e., our God does not consist of wood and tinsel, but He always remains an image, which is only another member of precisely the same series – subtler, but always an image. If the spirit of man wants to tear itself away from this worship of images, it finally arrives at the Kantian idea. But it is arrogance to believe that as mixed a being as man will ever acknowledge all that PURELY. Therefore, all that the really wise man can do is to guide everything towards a good goal, and yet to take men *as they are*. Of this Herr Fichte seems to understand nothing, and in this respect he is a rash and foolish man. – Forgive me, dear brother, I went further today than I intended. That's what happens when one's heart has a word to say too.

    Adieu, adieu.   G. C. L.

        * 'If you don't mind my saying so.'

SELECTED BIBLIOGRAPHY

A list of the principal works of Georg Christoph Lichtenberg
with the dates of their first appearance

VERMISCHTE SCHRIFTEN, 9 volumes (Dietrich, Göttingen, 1800–06)

VERMISCHTE SCHRIFTEN. VOLLSTÄNDIGE ORIGINALAUSGABE (Dieterich, Göttingen, vols 1–8 : 1844–7; vols 9–13 : 1850–53)

APHORISMEN, edited by A. Leitzmann, 5 volumes (B. Behr, Berlin, 1902–8)

BRIEFE, edited by A. Leitzmann and C. Schüddekopf, 3 volumes (Dieterich, Leipzig, 1901–4)

GESAMMELTE WERKE (Holle Verlag, Frankfurt am Main, 1949)

GEDANKENBÜCHER, edited by F. Mautner (Stiehm, Heidelberg, 1967)

Some translations from Lichtenberg

LICHTENBERG'S VISITS TO ENGLAND, Margaret L. Mare and W. H. Quarrell (Oxford, Clarendon Press, 1938)

THE LICHTENBERG READER, F. H. Mautner and H. Hatfield (Beacon Press, Boston, 1959)

LICHTENBERG'S COMMENTARIES ON HOGARTH'S ENGRAVINGS, G. and I. Herdan, Cresset Press, London, 1966)

THE AUTHOR

Georg Christoph Lichtenberg was born near Darmstadt in 1742. He lost his father at the age of nine. Marked by his small stature and the big hump on his back, he went to the University of Göttingen in 1763 to study astronomy, mathematics and physics; he earned his living as a tutor of English students. In 1770, he accompanied two of them on their way home and stayed one month in London. On his return, Lichtenberg was appointed Professor Extraordinarius at the University, but left for England again in 1774 and lived there for one and a half years. He was frequently the personal guest of George III, whom he had first met in 1770.

The first German chair of Experimental Physics was established for Lichtenberg after he had discovered, in 1777, an electrical phenomenon still called 'Lichtenberg's figures'. He was elected a member of the Royal Society and of the Petersburg Academy of Science. Prematurely aged, he declined a call to Leyden, then the centre of studies in Physics.

Lichtenberg also became well known as a writer. In *Letters from England* (1776–8) he dealt mainly with the English theatre. His *Detailed Explanation of Hogarth's Engravings* (1794–9) is still valued as the best topical commentary and is also a document of Lichtenberg's witty mind, as are his essays, causeries and pamphlets. He was founder-editor of the *Göttingisches Magazin der Wissenschaften und Literatur* (1780–85) and author-editor of the *Göttinger Taschenkalender* (since 1778), both of which were very influential. He suffered from melancholy and grave neuroses during his later years and died in 1799. His 'waste books', kept from his student days and found after his death, reveal that he anticipated twentieth-century depth psychology, linguistic analysis, and theory of knowledge.